Report on European-level Information and Consultation in Multinational Companies —

An Evaluation of Practice

EF/91/29/EN

**European Foundation
for the Improvement of
Living and Working Conditions**

Report on European-level Information and Consultation in Multinational Companies — An Evaluation of Practice

by

Michael Gold
London Management Centre
Polytechnic of Central London

and

Mark Hall
Industrial Relations Research Unit
University of Warwick

Loughlinstown House, Shankill, Co. Dublin, Ireland
Tel: 2826888 Fax: 2826456 Telex: 30726 EURF EI

European Communities—Commission

European-level Information and Consultation in Multinational Companies—
An Evaluation of Practice

Luxembourg: Office for Official Publications of the European Communities

1992—134p.—160 × 235mm

ISBN 92-826-3714-X

Catalogue Number: SY-73-91-522-EN-C

Price (excluding VAT) in Luxembourg: ECU 11.25

©Copyright: THE EUROPEAN FOUNDATION FOR THE IMPROVEMENT
OF LIVING AND WORKING CONDITIONS, 1992. For rights of translation or
reproduction, applications should be made to the Director, European Foundation
for Improvement of Living and Working Conditions, Loughlinstown, Shankill,
County Dublin, Ireland.

TABLE OF CONTENTS

PAGE

LIST OF TABLES		7
LIST OF KEY POINTS		7

1. **INTRODUCTION** — 9

    Background to this Report — 9
    The Research — 11
    Structure of the Report — 14

2. **EUROPEAN-LEVEL INFORMATION AND CONSULTATION BODIES WITHIN MULTINATIONALS: AN EMERGENT MODEL?** — 15

    Thomson Consumer Electronics — 15
    BSN — 18
    Bull — 20
    St Gobain — 21
    Péchiney — 21
    Rhône-Poulenc — 22
    Nestlé — 22
    Elf Aquitaine — 24
    Allianz — 24
    Volkswagen — 25
    Mercedes Benz — 26

    Comparison of Arrangements — 26
    A Basic Model — 28
    Variants — 35

3. **EVALUATION OF PRACTICE** — 37

    Origins of the Initiatives — 37
    Representation — 40
    Operational Aspects — 41
    Benefits to Management — 47
    Benefits to Employee Representatives — 48
    Negative Experiences — 51
    Future Development — 53
    Preconditions for Effectiveness — 57

4. **THE DRAFT EUROPEAN WORKS COUNCILS DIRECTIVE** — 59

    The Views of the Social Partners — 62

TABLE OF CONTENTS (continued)

				PAGE
5.	**SUMMARY AND CONCLUSION**			63
REFERENCES				67
SELECT BIBLIOGRAPHY				68
LIST OF ABBREVIATIONS				70
APPENDICES				71
	I	Company Profiles		71
	II	Key Documents		73
		Agreements	Bull	74
			Thomson	77
			- Liaison Committee	81
			- European Branch Committee	87
			Elf Aquitaine	103
		Exchange of Letters	BSN (Food & Drink)	112
			BSN (Glass)	
		Common Viewpoint	BSN (Food & Drink)	124
		Model Draft Agreements	EMF	127
			FIET	
	III	Current Situation at Airbus, CIS, Ford, Gillette, IBC and Unilever		129
	IV	Methodology		133

PAGE

LIST OF TABLES

Table 1	The Range of Company Arrangements	14
Table 2	Degrees of Formality in European-level Information/Consultation Arrangements	28
Table 3	Size/Composition of European-level Information/Consultation Arrangements	32
Table 4	European-level Information and Consultation Bodies - A Basic Model	34

LIST OF KEY POINTS

Management Rationales	39
Setting the Agenda	42
Feedback of Information	45
Benefits to Management	48
Benefits to Employee Representatives	51
Negative Experiences - Unions	53
Future Development	54
Attitudes towards Voluntary Agreements	56
Union Preconditions for Effectiveness	58
Conclusions	66

1. INTRODUCTION

The Background to this Report

This report is a revised and expanded version of a paper presented at the April 1991 Copenhagen Conference on 'Information and Consultation in European Multinationals' organised by the European Foundation for the Improvement of Living and Working Conditions, the Nordic Council of Ministers and the Nordic Foundation for Industrial Development. Conference delegates included management and union representatives, government officials and academics from some 15 European Community and Scandinavian countries.

The backdrop to the conference was the considerable interest shown in recent years in the spread of European-wide information and consultation arrangements within major multinational corporations. This interest has been prompted by a number of related factors, including moves within the European Community towards the single European market and economic and monetary union, the importance attached to the 'social dialogue' between the social partners (on the basis of Article 118B of the EC Treaty which was inserted by the Single European Act), and the development of European-level information and consultation bodies pioneered by Thomson, BSN and Bull during the second half of the 1980s. A crucial factor, however, is the renewed prospect of EC legislation requiring the establishment of European-level information and consultation procedures. In January 1991, the Commission of the European Communities published a draft directive on European Works Councils which was amended in September 1991. The directive, if implemented, would require all 'Community-scale' enterprises to establish some form of European-wide forum for the purposes of consulting with and providing information to employees. A separate initiative is the Commission's 1989 proposal for a European Company Statute under which 'European companies' operating on the basis of the proposed statute would also have to meet certain employee participation requirements. In February 1991, the Nordic Council decided to recommend the preparation of a proposal for coordinated Nordic legislation on group-level information and consultation procedures in groups of companies spanning several Nordic countries.

Of course, the European Community is not the only international organisation active in developing labour standards in this field. The 1976 OECD Declaration on International Investment and Multinational Enterprises includes guidelines which state that among other things multinationals should:

* provide employee representatives with information on the performance of the local subsidiary or, where appropriate, the multinational as a whole;

* provide reasonable notice of changes in the company's operations likely to have major effects on the livelihood of their employees, and to cooperate to mitigate adverse effects;

* not threaten to transfer the company's operations from one country to another in order to influence negotiations or inhibit employees' right to organise; and

* enable employee representatives to negotiate with managers 'authorised to take decisions on the matters under negotiation'.

Provisions similar to certain of these are also included in the 1977 ILO Tripartite Declaration of Principles concerning Multinational Enterprises and Social Policy. The ILO Declaration also states that:

'Representatives of the workers in multinational enterprises should not be hindered from meeting for consultation and exchange of views among themselves, provided that the functioning of the operations of the enterprise and the normal procedures which govern relationships with representatives of the workers and their organisations are not thereby prejudiced.'

A more recent international instrument of relevance, though not aimed specifically at multinationals, is the 1987 Additional Protocol to the Council of Europe's European Social Charter. This promotes the provision of information about the economic and financial situation of undertakings, and consultation in good time on proposed decisions which could substantially affect the interests of workers, particularly those which could have an important impact on employment.

However influential such international instruments may or may not be, they essentially take the form of guidelines, the observance of which by multinational corporations is voluntary. EC members states, on the other hand, are obliged to comply with the terms of EC directives, and effective means of enforcement exist through the European Court of Justice. The significance of the proposed EC legislation, therefore, is that multinational corporations could eventually face the direct, binding and legally enforceable regulation of their information and consultation practices through legislation in EC member states implementing the European Works Councils directive.

The Research

The research project on which this report is based was sponsored by the European Foundation for the Improvement of Living and Working Conditions, and had the aim of producing an overview of European-wide information and consultation arrangements within multinationals in the European Community. In particular, the terms of reference from the Foundation directed the researchers to:

* provide a systematic comparison of existing formal, informal or proposed arrangements within European multinationals;

* evaluate the practice of European-wide information/consultation on the basis of management and employee-side views on their operation; and

* compare existing agreements and practice with the provisions of the proposed EC directive on European Works Councils adopted by the Commission in December 1990.

With these objectives in view, the report outlines the findings of what is a preliminary study. The study involved 35 semi-structured interviews with management, trade union and employee representatives in the following 15 companies (on which background information is presented in tabular form in Appendix I):

*	Airbus	*	Nestlé
*	Allianz	*	Péchiney
*	BSN Group	*	Rhône-Poulenc
*	Bull	*	St Gobain
*	Cooperative Insurance Society	*	Thomson Consumer Electronics
*	Ford	*	Unilever
*	Gillette	*	Volkswagen
*	IBC		

The Cooperative Insurance Society, though not itself a multinational company, is the British affiliate of the Association of European Cooperative Insurers (AECI), which is party to a long-standing *sectoral* European-level information/consultation arrangement involving Euro-FIET. IBC is a joint venture established between General Motors and Isuzu.

A further eight interviews were carried out with representatives of the following European-level employers' and trade union organisations:

Employers:
- * Council of European Chemical Federations (CEFIC)
- * Union of Industrial and Employers' Confederations of Europe (UNICE)
- * Western European Metal Trades Employers' Organisation

Unions:
- * European Committee of Food, Catering and Allied Workers' Unions within the IUF (ECF/IUF)
- * European Federation of Chemical and General Workers' Unions (EFCGU)
- * European Metalworkers' Federation in the Community (EMF)
- * European Regional Organisation of the International Federation of Commercial, Clerical and Technical Employees (Euro-FIET)
- * European Trade Union Confederation (ETUC)

In addition to carrying out the interviews listed, we have analysed documentation relating to the information/consultation arrangements where available (such as copies of collective agreements). Key documents are reproduced in Appendix II.

As already noted, considerable attention has been paid to the European-level information/consultation committees pioneered by the French-based multinational groups Thomson, BSN and Bull during the second half of the 1980s. Similar or analogous arrangements were found to be operating in nine of the fifteen companies investigated - Allianz, BSN, Bull, Nestlé, Péchiney, Rhône-Poulenc, St Gobain, Thomson and Volkswagen.

In none of the six remaining companies investigated was there a European-level, workforce-wide information/consultation forum. The Cooperative Insurance Society participates in European-level information/consultation meetings, but this is a sectoral, multi-employer arrangement. Within Ford (in the product development area) and IBC, there are joint exchange visits between European plants and similar visits also take place between IBC and General Motors plants. At Airbus, Gillette and Unilever, no European-level joint meetings take place. Union attempts to secure the establishment of European-level management/employee-side contact within these three companies and Ford have not yet been successful.

The range of different arrangements which apply in the companies investigated is summarised below in Table 1; details of the nine companies located in band A are discussed in more depth in Section 2, whilst details of those located in bands B, C and D (where developments are either marginal or currently deadlocked) are discussed in Appendix III.

The purpose of the research was to enable a *qualitative* evaluation of the operation of European-level information/consultation arrangements, not to assess the *extent* of such arrangements. Thus, the companies investigated are not a random set. They are, rather, companies known to be involved in some form of established European-wide information/consultation arrangements, or companies where an attempt is being made to establish such an arrangement. We do not claim to have produced an exhaustive list of companies with such arrangements. On the contrary, we are aware that there are other companies where similar developments have taken place or may be under consideration. For example, the agreement at Elf Aquitaine and the establishment of a European employee representation committee within Mercedes Benz, which are referred to in Section 2, postdate our programme of interviews. Meanwhile, the Scandinavian experience in this area, including developments at Scansped, has been studied by Gunnar Myrvang[1].

Further details of the methodology are given in Appendix IV.

Table 1: The Range of Company Arrangements

A.	**COMPANY/GROUP-WIDE EUROPEAN-LEVEL JOINT INFORMATION/CONSULTATION FORUM**

Allianz Rhône-Poulenc
BSN St Gobain
Bull Thomson
Nestlé Volkswagen
Péchiney

B.	**PARTY TO SECTORAL EUROPEAN-LEVEL JOINT INFORMATION/CONSULTATION ARRANGEMENTS**

Cooperative Insurance Society

C.	**JOINT EXCHANGE VISITS BETWEEN EUROPEAN PLANTS**

Ford   IBC

D.	**NO TRANSNATIONAL JOINT MEETINGS**

Airbus   Unilever
Gillette

The Structure of the Report

Section 2 of the report analyses the structural aspects of a number of European-level information/consultation bodies. Section 3 evaluates the practices operated in the companies investigated, whilst Section 4 examines the relationship between existing arrangements and the provisions of the proposed European Works Councils directive. The main conclusions of the report are summarised in Section 5.

2. EUROPEAN-LEVEL INFORMATION AND CONSULTATION BODIES WITHIN MULTINATIONALS: AN EMERGENT MODEL?

This Section of the report outlines and compares the composition, competence and procedural characteristics of the European-level information/consultation bodies within multinational corporations identified by our research, plus two other such arrangements (at Elf Aquitaine and Mercedes Benz). The material is presented broadly in chronological order, with the oldest established arrangements first, and the French examples, plus Nestlé, preceding the German.

It should be noted at the outset that whereas the European-level information/consultation bodies at Thomson, BSN (Food and Drink) and Bull are well-established and reasonably well-documented arrangements, others are much more recent and in some cases based on informal understandings. Our analysis, therefore, focuses in particular on those cases where detailed documentary material has been available to us (through collective agreements and so on). We then go on to discuss the extent to which it is possible to talk about the emergence of a basic model for European-level information/consultation structures within multinational companies.

Thomson Consumer Electronics

Within Thomson Consumer Electronics (which was known until January 1989 as Thomson Grand Public), two parallel European-level information and consultation bodies have operated since 1 January 1986 - the Thomson Consumer Electronics/European Metalworkers' Federation Liaison Committee (Comité de liaison), and the Thomson Consumer Electronics European Branch Committee (Commission de branche européenne). The first of these, as its name suggests, is a liaison body between Thomson management and representatives of the trade unions affiliated to the EMF. The European Branch Committee, on the other hand, comprises Thomson employees nominated by the unions from among the selected members of works councils or similar bodies. Both bodies are subject to separate formal written agreements between management and unions signed on 7 October 1985, initially for a two-year period only. However, subsequent agreements extended both bodies for an indefinite period from 1

January 1988 (the agreement covering the Liaison Committee was signed on 22 December 1987 while the one covering the European Branch Committee was signed on 6 April 1988). At the same time, in each case, British representation was added. Further agreements to adjust membership were signed on 18 December 1989 and 19 January 1990 respectively. Nine months' notice is required to modify either agreement.

The current agreement on the composition of the Liaison Committee provides for a trade union side of 12 members, one seat being reserved for a representative of the EMF and the remaining 11 seats being allocated to national unions affiliated to the EMF. The Thomson group is represented by senior management including the Managing Director. The committee meets every six months at the initiative of either side, but there is provision for ad hoc meetings, perhaps in 'restricted form', where agreed by both parties. It is also provided that the annual meeting must precede the annual session of the Thomson European Branch Committee. The interpretation costs are met by the group as are the travelling and accommodation expenses and wages of those members of the Liaison Committee who are group employees.

In terms of formal competence, the Liaison Committee is essentially for information purposes, though members of the committee may 'express opinions' on the information supplied. The agreement provides that the Liaison Committee shall be informed of:

* the economic, industrial, trading and research activities of the group;

* major structural, industrial and trading modifications and changes in the economic and legal organisation of the group prior to their implementation; and

* measures taken and planned for adapting the organisation and workforce to technological change as well as adapting employees' skills in the light of employment problems.

The agreement also provides for the EMF to have access to the documents transmitted to the Thomson European Branch Committee, but it must respect the confidential or secret nature of these documents vis-à-vis third parties.

The Thomson European Branch Committee is composed of senior management representatives and 20 staff representatives drawn from among the elected members of works councils or similar bodies who are designated by representative trade unions in the countries concerned (or, failing this, by works councils). Each country where the group operates is allocated two seats with the remainder being distributed in proportion to the number of employees in each country.

The Committee meets once a year at the initiative of the management, but may also meet on an ad hoc basis for 'any problem likely to modify the industrial or commercial situation at European level'. The group guarantees the staff representatives' wages and also meets the costs of the meeting room and interpretation, travel and living expenses.

The mandate of members of the Committee lasts two years, after which a new allocation of seats is made according to prevailing circumstances. The agreement states that changes to the membership of the Committee during the two-year mandate should not be made except where the person concerned leaves the group's employment, ceases to be a member of the local works council or relevant committee or, in the case of Germany, loses the confidence of the central or works council concerned.

The competence of the Thomson European Branch Committee is confined to the provision of information on issues broadly comparable to those identified in the Liaison Committee agreement. It is to be informed of:

* the economic, industrial, commercial and research activities of the group in Europe, and measures taken or envisaged so as to adapt staff to developments in technology and to adapt their qualifications in the face of employment problems;

* major structural or industrial changes, in advance, when decision are taken at group level; and

* any changes in the organisation of the group (for example, the purchase or sale of subsidiaries).

BSN

Within the BSN Group, a European Consultation Committee (Comité européen de consultation) covering its food and drink division has been operating since March 1987 on the basis of an agreement reached between the group and the IUF and its European Committee on 29 October 1986. Unlike the Thomson arrangement, the BSN European Consultation Committee is not the subject of a formal written collective agreement. The terms on which the Committee was established were, however, the subject of discussions between management and unions, and were made official by means of an exchange of letters between the two parties in June 1986[2].

The Committee is composed of:

* the ECF and IUF secretariats plus the secretaries of the competent national member organisations (15 people in all); and

* 15 delegates from BSN plants in Europe, nominated by the national unions, taking account of the different sectors.

There are annual meetings of the Committee, normally held in April, the preparations for which are made by a smaller working group of ECF/IUF representatives and BSN management. Where necessary, meetings of the working group or ad hoc bilateral meetings may take place between the annual meetings[3]. BSN covers the costs of the venue, interpreting and expenses of the 15 BSN employees, who are also given paid time off work to attend the meetings.

This arrangement was originally intended to run for a two-year experimental period, but after the second annual meeting (in 1988) the parties agreed to continue the meetings of the European Consultation Committee. Another outcome of the contacts between ECF/IUF and BSN was the 'common viewpoint' (avis commun) signed by the two parties in August 1988. This set out four areas on which BSN and ECF/IUF had decided to work jointly:

* skills training to anticipate the consequences of new technology and industrial restructuring;

* the harmonisation of the level and quantity of economic and social information made available by BSN subsidiaries;

* equality between men and women at work; and

* the development of trade union rights.

On 3 April 1990, BSN management agreed, on an experimental basis, the final details of a European Information Committee in respect of its glass division (Commission d'information verrière européenne) with union representatives from France, the Netherlands and Spain. The details were confirmed in an exchange of letters. This committee had been requested by the French CGT and the Spanish CNT in 1988, following the 100% takeover of the Spanish company Vidreria Vilella by BSN. The first meeting of this Committee took place on 10 October 1990 in Seville.

The framework for this institution is again set out by letter rather than in a formal collective agreement. The letter[4] from BSN management to the unions concerned following a meeting where the arrangements were discussed makes clear that the purpose of the Committee is to enable the participants to receive and exchange information concerning economic and social developments in BSN's glass subsidiaries (results, markets, industrial plans, technological innovation, conditions of work, safety and training). The participants are able to propose agenda items for the Committee, and documents making comparisons between the different BSN glass processing concerns are prepared. However, it is stressed in the letter that the Committee is in no way a forum for negotiation and must not encroach on representative arrangements which exist within each subsidiary.

The Committee comprises 12 representatives of BSN's glass concerns, nominated by the appropriate trade unions, plus senior BSN management. There is paid time off for those attending the meeting, and BSN also meets their travel and accommodation expenses. Interpretation facilities were made available to the trade union side for a preparatory meeting the day before the first meeting of the Committee.

Bull

An agreement setting up the Bull European Information Committee (Comité d'information européen de Bull) was signed by the group and five representative French trade unions on 22 March 1988. The agreement, which took effect initially for two years from 1 May 1988, was for a two-year trial period and provided for two meetings during its lifetime. Negotiations on the renewal of the agreement are understood to be continuing.

Described as 'a European information and consultation body for the purpose of establishing a dialogue in the European countries in which Bull is located', the Committee is now made up of 28 shop stewards/lay representatives from 14 countries, five more representatives (two from the UK, three from Italy) having been added in 1989, though they are not mentioned in the agreement. This move followed Bull's acquisition of Honeywell and part of Olivetti in 1987. The agreement leaves the method of appointment to negotiations in each of the countries concerned. It states that: 'These negotiations will take into account current legislation in each of the countries concerned and will give rise to the signature of an additional clause to the agreement signed by the management of each [subsidiary] company and the trade union representatives, or failing this staff representatives.'

Under the agreement employee representatives are able to hold a preparatory meeting prior to each meeting of the Committee. The Bull Group management meets the travel and accommodation costs incurred by the employee representatives. The agreement stipulates that the information supplied at meetings of the Committee will 'relate to trading, economic, financial and social matters in respect of the whole group' and will be followed by 'an exchange of views and discussions'.

St Gobain

Meetings between European unions represented in St Gobain and group-level management have taken place sporadically since 1983, but regularly since 1989. Since then, management has organised an annual meeting for European unions (une réunion des syndicats européens) to which it invites around 70 trade unionists from the ten European countries in which it has subsidiaries. There is no agreement on the format or constitution of meetings, which are informal. Management sets the principal themes for discussion: in 1989, the meeting held in Paris focused on training; in 1990, in Brussels, on safety; and in 1991, in Ludwigshafen, on quality.

St Gobain, whilst insisting that it does not have a European group committee (Comité de groupe européen), nevertheless affirms its intention of continuing the formula of an annual meeting which allows not only two-way exchanges of information between management and unions but also, as the company itself points out, exchanges between the unions themselves.

Péchiney

In June 1990 management reached an agreement with the five major French union confederations to establish a European Information Committee (Commission européenne d'information) with Péchiney. As far as we are aware, this is a verbal agreement only, although a document outlining the composition and other aspects of the Committee's organisation does exist. This Committee is seen as an exercise in 'information, reflection and exchange' with the aim of developing the dialogue between central management and employee representatives about the position and strategies concerning the principal areas of activity within the Péchiney group. The Committee is to receive information on the position and direction of the group in the different areas of activity within the EC, and on the evolution of the group's activities in other countries.

The Committee is composed of 28 employee representatives designated in the case of France by representative trade union organisations and in the other European countries in which Péchiney operates by the appropriate representative bodies of the employees in the subsidiaries concerned. There is to be one plenary meeting per year paid for by

Péchiney. The first took place in June 1990 and the second in April 1991. The mandate of the employee representatives lasts two years, and their wages are guaranteed by the company during their attendance at the Committee.

Rhône-Poulenc

Management at Rhône-Poulenc took the initiative to hold a joint meeting in Paris between themselves and 35 employees or employee representatives from the six EC member states in which the company has plants. This first meeting took place on 22 November 1990 and it is likely to be followed by others on an annual basis. Management issued its own invitations to the meeting and there was no agreement of any kind in relation to its format or constitution. No committee system is envisaged. In 1989, when Rhône-Poulenc took over RTZ Chemicals, the UK union MSF approached the company for information on corporate strategy, but was apparently rebuffed. Following this, MSF began to develop its own links with the French union confederations, CGT and CFDT, to discuss common objectives. In addition, 150 delegates attended an international conference of trade unions representing Rhône-Poulenc workers on 21/22 June 1990 hosted by the CGT at their headquarters at Montreuil. In the light of this, the unions believe that the meeting held on 22 November was an attempt to counteract their own activities.

Nestlé

Following its success in establishing a European consultation committee within the BSN Group in 1986, the International Union of Foodworkers (IUF) approached Nestlé for a similar arrangement. However, the initiative for the first meeting, we understand, resulted from personal contact between a senior representative of the German foodworkers' union, NGG, and the President of Nestlé Europe, who reacted favourably in the context of the development of the single European market.

The first IUF/Nestlé meeting, as it was called, took place in Geneva on 10 December 1990. However, these meetings are based on a confidential exchange of letters and no committee system has been established.

German law and practice is the presence of both German and French employee representatives on Europipe's supervisory board.

The report has also evaluated the operation of these arrangements in nine of the multinationals where they exist. The management and employee representatives interviewed who were party to such arrangements were generally satisfied with their operation. For example, managers stressed their value in facilitating restructuring within the company and promoting an international corporate identity. Employee representatives emphasised among other things the importance of developing international contacts and gathering group-wide information which could then be used in domestic collective bargaining. However, as we saw in Section 3, neither side was uncritical either. Both managements and unions have views about the future development of these arrangements, and the unions listed a series of negative experiences, such as the infrequency of meetings and problems in following up issues. Their preconditions for effectiveness included the need for preparatory meetings, strategy for the use of information and research support.

Notwithstanding the relatively small number - and narrow range - of multinational companies in which European-level information/consultation arrangements currently operate, their existence would appear to have exerted a powerful influence on European Community policy-making. Our analysis has drawn attention to the similarities between such arrangements and the provisions of the proposed European Works Councils directive, along with some important differences. Overall, however, these 'prototype European Works Councils' represent a valuable testing ground for many aspects of the European Commission's proposals, and our findings concerning their operation provide some indication of the likely impact of the directive if implemented. However, in present circumstances, in view of the directive's legal basis (which requires unanimity on the Council of Ministers) and the stated opposition to the directive of the United Kingdom, there would seem to be little possibility of the early adoption of the current text, other things being equal.

What, then, are the prospects for the continued spread of European-level information and consultation arrangements within multinational corporations *without* legislative backing in the form of the European Works Council directive? To the extent that managements perceive that the existence of such arrangements may constrain a

The body comprises Elf Aquitaine's senior management, 30 employee representatives from French subsidiaries and 45 employee representatives from Elf Aquitaine's other European subsidiaries. The French employee representatives must be group employees and are to be designated by the trade unions from among existing elected employee representatives or lay union officials. Each of the five major French trade union confederations is entitled to nominate one employee representative for each of the three group divisions (a total of fifteen). The remaining fifteen posts are determined in proportion to the results of the latest elections for employee representatives on the Board of Directors of Société Nationale Elf Aquitaine.

For the non-French Elf subsidiaries, employee representatives and, 'if in keeping with local procedures', the delegates of union organisations represented in the company, may make nominations for appointment to the European Information and Concertation Body. If the number of candidates is greater than the number of seats to be filled, the representatives will be elected either by a vote of all employee representatives or by a vote of the employees themselves. The 45 available seats are allocated in order to ensure that the different group divisions should be equally represented with fifteen representatives per division, and that for any different division each country employing at least 50 people will be represented by one or more delegates.

Allianz

Some years ago Euro-FIET established an international trade union council within Allianz, Europe's largest insurance company, known as the Allianz Company Council. It meets every year - most recently in Stuttgart in 1988, in Bishops Stortford in 1989, and in Munich in 1990. Euro-FIET invites management each year to attend these meetings and in both 1989 and 1990 senior management did, indeed, attend and give a presentation (in 1990 at Allianz headquarters in Munich on the occasion of the company's centenary). However, management has made it clear that it will attend only at its own discretion and without prejudice to its future position. Euro-FIET has drawn up a model agreement for a European Information Committee but Allianz has steadfastly refused to discuss it.

Volkswagen

On 30 August 1990, an agreement between the various company-level employee representative bodies of European companies within the Volkswagen group established the European Volkswagen Group Works Council (Europäischer Volkswagen-Gesamtbetriebsrat). It comprises eight members from Volkswagen AG, two from Audi AG, five from SEAT (Volkswagen's Spanish subsidiary), and two from VW Brussels. This makes a total of 17 members, who elect from their number a President, General Secretary and Presidium with at least one member from each country.

The agreement states that only freely-elected and democratically legitimised company-level employee representatives in Volkswagen companies in individual countries where legislation provides for adequate representation may become members of the European Volkswagen Group Works Council. It also states that 'procedures for delegating members to the European Volkswagen Group Works Council shall be the subject of special regulation in the individual national parts of the Volkswagen group. This may, where appropriate, also include the setting up of coordinating bodies at national level'.

The European Volkswagen Group Works Council is convened at least once a year by its Presidium to 'exchange information and work out joint positions, in particular on the following issues, provided that at least two national groups are affected :-

* security of employment and of local operations and local structures
* developments in group structure
* trends in working time
* trends in working conditions
* rationalisation through use of new technology
* new forms of work organisation
* pay
* health and safety and environmental protection
* social provision
* policy developments and decisions'.

Such joint decisions are to be conveyed to Volkswagen's group management.

The agreement also states that 'members of the European Volkswagen Group Works Council shall commit themselves to upholding the spirit of the joint decisions in national plants and companies' and to 'joint action and solidarity on all issues of supranational significance which affect the interests of workforces elsewhere'. The Group Works Council will cooperate with the EMF and with 'all democratic and representative trade unions in the plants and companies of Volkswagen'. Trade union representatives from outside the company may be invited to attend meetings. Similarly, 'advisers from the company or from outside bodies' may also be invited to meetings.

On costs, the agreement states that 'the group and individual companies shall bear the costs of the European Volkswagen Group Works Council's work. An agreement on this point shall be concluded with the board of Volkswagen AG'.

VW management meets the European Group Works Council but only at its own discretion. Whilst it has adopted a cooperative attitude, it has given no commitment to continue participating in meetings and opposes a more formal joint information/consultation arrangement.

Mercedes Benz

At a meeting on 11 and 12 March 1991, delegates from employee representative bodies in Mercedes Benz plants outside Germany approved the constitution of a European Employee Representative Committee for the company (Comité européen des représentants du personnel/europäischer Ausschuss für Personalvertretungen). The board of the parent company subsequently 'indicated its intention to give employee representatives in the various countries the opportunity to attend an international exchange of views on an annual basis'[5]. The next meeting of the Mercedes Benz European Employee Representative Committee is scheduled to take place in Italy in early 1992, with the support of the management of Mercedes Benz Italia.

Comparison of Arrangements

A comparison of the key characteristics of the bodies discussed above reveals many similarities in approach, but also some important differences.

One difference at the outset is the degree of *formalisation* with which the structures and procedures for European-level information and consultation have been agreed between the parties. As we have seen, the arrangements within Bull, Elf Aquitaine and Thomson Consumer Electronics are based on formal written agreements or contracts. Yet in three other companies - BSN, Nestlé and Péchiney - the arrangements now operating have been discussed and agreed with the trade unions representing their employees, but are not the subject of a formal written agreement. The two information bodies at BSN and the Nestlé arrangement are based on an exchange of letters. At Péchiney there is, we understand, a verbal agreement with the five major French trade unions concerned. Therefore, it is possible to distinguish between those arrangements which are the subject of *formal written agreement* and those which can be described as being an *agreed practice*; that is, where there is no formal written agreement but where the arrangement has been determined through negotiation and agreement between management and unions/employee representatives.

The other arrangements considered in this Section are examples of either management or employee initiatives which in practice receive informal support, or at least cooperation, from the other party. These we have termed *informal arrangements*. Thus, at Rhône-Poulenc and St Gobain, central management invites employee representatives to an annual European-level information meeting whose subject matter is determined by management. Allianz and Volkswagen are examples of companies which have adopted an even more non-committal stance; cooperating informally with union initiatives but only, it seems, on a meeting-by-meeting basis and without wishing to prejudice their future policy. At Mercedes Benz, employee initiatives, with apparently some informal support from management, have prompted the company to propose an annual international forum for the exchange of views.

This approach to distinguishing between the European-level information/consultation arrangements covered by the research is represented in Table 2.

These distinctions, however, are very fluid. For example, we might ask at what point an informal arrangement becomes agreed practice - at what point does Volkswagen management's willingness to attend meetings of the employee-convened European Group Works Council, or the employee representatives' participation in Rhône-Poulenc management's annual information meetings, become a form of agreed practice? Nevertheless, we believe that the distinction between informal arrangements and agreed practice is a significant one as it focuses attention on the basis, and therefore the stability, of the arrangement.

Table 2: Degrees of Formality in European-level Information/Consultation Arrangements

FORMAL WRITTEN AGREEMENT	AGREED PRACTICE	INFORMAL ARRANGEMENT	
		Initiated by management	Initiated by employee representatives
Bull	BSN (Food and Drink)	Rhône-Poulenc	Allianz
Elf Aquitaine	BSN (Glass)	St Gobain	Mercedes Benz
Thomson Consumer Electronics:	Nestlé		Volkswagen
- Liaison Committee	Péchiney		
- European Branch Committee			

A Basic Model

Notwithstanding the different degrees of formalisation exhibited by the European information/consultation arrangements under consideration - and despite the limited number of such arrangements established to date - it is possible to identify a set of key characteristics or core provisions with which all the jointly agreed arrangements are broadly consistent (that is, those arrangements which are the subject of formal written agreements plus those which are agreed practices). With the exception of Swiss-owned Nestlé, all the companies concerned are French-based, and the key characteristics of their European-level information and consultation arrangements appear to reflect the influence of domestic employee participation legislation in France.

As regards the *competence* of the jointly agreed European-level bodies, most are essentially informational in character - that is to say their role is confined to receiving and discussing information provided by the group's management. Nevertheless, it is true that the Bull agreement refers to the Bull European Information Committee as an 'information and consultation committee for the purpose of establishing a dialogue' and provides that information 'will be followed by an exchange of views and discussions'.

The Elf Aquitaine agreement, too, is intended to 'promote ... a constructive social dialogue based ... on information and consultation of workers'. Similarly, members of the Thomson Consumer Electronics/ EMF Liaison Committee may 'express opinions' and the Péchiney arrangement is also described in terms of 'dialogue'. In this report, therefore, we have tended to refer generally to European 'information and consultation' bodies. Yet, in the more formal sense of 'consultation' as embodied in the legislation of a number of EC member states, they cannot properly be regarded as consultation bodies: there is no staged consultation procedure whereby employers provide the relevant information about proposed changes, the works council then forms and expresses an opinion with a view to influencing the decision, and the employer subsequently responds to the points raised by the works council[6]. The exception would appear to be BSN (Food and Drink) where European-level meetings have gone further and resulted in a programme of joint work covering a number of important areas of industrial relations policy.

A proposed agreement under consideration in 1988 between the EMF and Continental Can (but never, so far as we are aware, concluded) would have given employee representatives '30 days in which to consider management proposals affecting employment, with the benefit of outside expert counsel'. Such an agreement would thus have gone 'beyond mere information and strengthened the consultative rights of the employee representatives'[7]. Moreover, a provision of this nature would be consistent with the EMF's model agreement for establishing European-level information and consultation committees[8] (reproduced in Appendix II). This provides that there should be a right to consultation over a range of issues including rationalisation plans, organisational change, and other developments or plans which may substantially affect employees. The EMF document states that :

> 'If measures likely to affect the interests of the workforce in more than one country are being contemplated, the European information body should be consulted before any decision is taken. Should this body perceive any adverse effects for the workforce, any decision shall be postponed for a predetermined period, at its request, in order to allow time for a compromise to be worked out, if necessary with the assistance of experts specially called in for this purpose.'

A model agreement drawn up by Euro-FIET aimed at establishing a 'European Information Committee' in multinational companies (also reproduced in Appendix II) states that such a committee 'is intended to promote regular consultation on issues of mutual concern', but like the existing arrangements this appears to be envisaged in terms of an 'exchange [of] views and information' and no specific consultation procedure is put forward.

As well as reflecting management's efforts to limit the scope and influence of European-level bodies, the 'information-only' characteristic of most existing bodies also owes something to the fact that the 1982 French legislation on group enterprise committees (comités de groupe) is confined to the right to information.

A related point is that discussion is confined to *group-level issues*. This is made clear in the Thomson and Bull agreements, but the point is put most explicitly in the BSN letter setting out the arrangements for the establishment of the new European Information Committee in its glass operations. As already noted, this warns that the new body must not encroach on representative arrangements which exist within each BSN subsidiary company. On this point the EMF model agreement stresses that:

> 'The role of these information bodies is to complement similar bodies existing at national level. Under no circumstances should they replace the latter. The national rights of worker representatives in the various countries will remain unchanged'.

A similar clause is contained in Article (1) of the Elf Aquitaine agreement.

Another key issue is the method of *employee representation* on the jointly agreed European-level bodies. Provision is made for the participation of trade union officers in the BSN, Nestlé and Thomson (Liaison Committee) arrangements whereas they are not included in the other bodies we have looked at. However, even where it is specified that the members of such bodies must be group employees, it is the trade unions which operate within the group which generally have the right to designate who they should be from among existing employee representatives within group enterprises. (The possible exceptions to this pattern are Bull, where the agreement leaves the issue to negotiation in each different country, and Péchiney, where the non-French members are designated by the appropriate representative bodies of the employees in the subsidiaries concerned.) Thus, there is generally an intersection between the appropriate trade union organisations and internal company employee representation arrangements (frequently works councils) in respect of nominations to the European-level body which would appear to offer a valuable mechanism for ensuring the acceptability of the European-level body to both organs of employee representation.

It should also be noted that, like the French works councils (comités d'entreprise) the jointly agreed European-level information/consultation arrangements involve a *joint management/employee forum* - whether a formal ongoing committee structure (for example, in the case of Bull, Thomson, BSN, Péchiney and Elf Aquitaine) or ad hoc annual meetings (Nestlé).

The relatively small *size* of most existing European-level information and consultation bodies is also a notable feature (see Table 3). The number of employee representatives on such bodies ranges from 12 in the cases of BSN (Glass) and Thomson (Liaison Committee) up to 75 in the case of Elf Aquitaine. However, most of the jointly agreed arrangements we have looked at involve fewer than 30 employee representatives - the figure specified in the French legislation for group enterprise committees (the exceptions are Elf Aquitaine and Swiss-owned Nestlé). The groups examined are all major European employers with large numbers of subsidiaries and individual plants, and this means that not all enterprises within the group will have representatives on the European-level body, but it is clearly important to have a forum of manageable proportions.

As regards *procedure*, annual meetings are the norm, though the Thomson, BSN and Elf Aquitaine arrangements also envisage possible ad hoc meetings of the bodies concerned. Preparatory meetings of the employee representatives are facilitated under the Bull, Elf Aquitaine and Nestlé arrangements, and the annual meetings of the BSN Consultation Committee are prepared by a joint management-union working group.

TABLE 3: SIZE/COMPOSITION OF EUROPEAN-LEVEL INFORMATION/CONSULTATION ARRANGEMENTS

COMPANY	NAME OF BODY	MANAGEMENT REPRESENTATION	EMPLOYEE REPRESENTATION - FULL TIME OFFICIALS	EMPLOYEE REPRESENTATION - EMPLOYEE REPS (NOMINATED THROUGH WORKS COUNCIL OR UNION)	PRESENCE OF REPRESENTATIVE FROM EUROPEAN INDUSTRY COMMITTEE	TOTAL
Allianz	Allianz Company Council	Senior management, such as the Personnel Director, attends at its own discretion	Not fixed	-	✓	20-25
BSN Group	European Consultation Committee (Food and Drink)	5-10 General Manager, divisional managers and assistants	15	15	✓	30
BSN Group	European Information Committee (Glass Division)	Chairman/MD of the division and Human Resources Directors from each country	-	12	-	12
Bull Group	Bull European Information Committee	5-6 Chairman, MD, senior executives	-	28	-	28
Elf Aquitaine	European Information and Concertation Body	8 Chairman and Chief Executive Officer, 3 Senior Vice Presidents and Chief Operating Officer from each of the three group divisions	-	-	-	75
Nestlé	IUF/Nestlé meeting	21 President of Nestlé Europe, heads of European operations, Director of Human Resources and Personnel Directors from each country	16	30	4	50

TABLE 3: SIZE/COMPOSITION OF EUROPEAN-LEVEL INFORMATION/CONSULTATION ARRANGEMENTS

COMPANY	NAME OF BODY	MANAGEMENT REPRESENTATION	EMPLOYEE REPRESENTATION – FULL TIME OFFICIALS	EMPLOYEE REPRESENTATION – EMPLOYEE REPS (NOMINATED THROUGH WORKS COUNCIL OR UNION)	PRESENCE OF REPRESENTATIVE FROM EUROPEAN INDUSTRY COMMITTEE	TOTAL
Péchiney	European Information Committee	5 – Chairman and MD Péchiney, General Manager and Assistant General Manager, Social Affairs Manager	-	28	-	28
Rhône-Poulenc	Joint meeting ("une instance de dialogue social")	9 – Chairman, MD and Director of Social Affairs for the Group, 3 Personnel Directors, 3 General Managers	-	-	-	35
St Gobain	Joint meeting ("une réunion des syndicats européens")	4-5 – Chairman, General Manager, Assistant Directors of Social Affairs and of Human Resources	-	-	-	70
Thomson Consumer Electronics	Liaison Committee	MD together with relevant Directors	11	-	1	12
Thomson Consumer Electronics	European Branch Committee	Chairmans and MD of Thomson Consumer Electronics plus relevant directors	-	20	-	20
Volkswagen	European Volkswagen Group Works Council	Management attends at its own discretion	-	17	-	17

It is also the norm that the group meets the *costs* of the meetings (venue, interpretation, and so on), pays travel and accommodation expenses of at least those participants who are group employees (as opposed to union full-time officials), and grants paid time off to group employees taking part in the meetings.

Only in the agreement establishing the Thomson/EMF Liaison Committee is the confidentiality of the information provided to employee representatives the subject of a specific provision, though a confidentiality clause also features in the FIET model agreement.

Finally, a further notable feature concerns the *duration* of the agreements or arrangements. The Thomson, BSN and Bull committees were all initially established for a two-year trial period. In each case the arrangements have subsequently been continued for an indefinite period. The recent Elf Aquitaine agreement is also for an initial two-year period.

Pulling together these common features of the jointly agreed European-level information arrangements currently operating in a number of French-based multinationals, it is possible to construct a basic model. This is summarised in Table 4, and as has already been noted it reflects the strong influence of French law and practice.

Table 4: European-level Information and Consultation Bodies - A Basic Model

Competence
* Information only
* Group-level issues

Representation
* Joint management/employee bodies
* Intersection of trade union/employee representation
* Relatively small number of participants

Procedure
* Annual meetings
* Group meets costs

Duration
* Initial trial period

Variants

While the two management-initiated informal arrangements (Rhône-Poulenc and St. Gobain) share some of these characteristics, the number of employee representatives participating in the ad hoc annual meetings held by both companies is in each case higher than 30 (35 at Rhône-Poulenc; 70 at St. Gobain). In addition, Rhône-Poulenc issues its own invitations to selected employee representatives rather than allowing the trade unions to make the nominations.

The informal arrangements initiated by employee representatives at Allianz, Volkswagen and Mercedes Benz - all German-based companies - also differ from the basic, French-influenced model.

The existing European-wide bodies in these companies - Euro-FIET's Allianz Company Council, the Mercedes Benz European Employee Representative Committee and the European Volkswagen Group Works Council - are employee/trade union-only bodies, not joint employee/management bodies. Furthermore, within Volkswagen at least, the role of the European body goes beyond the exchange of information and includes the 'adoption of joint positions' (Abstimmung gemeinsamer Positionen) on transnational matters which members of the European Volkswagen Group Works Council are committed to uphold at national company/plant level.

It is possible to speculate that these features are a reflection of German works councils law and practice. However, in each case the employee representatives and trade unions concerned are seeking from company management the establishment of a formal joint European-level information/consultation body. At Allianz and Volkswagen, this continues to be resisted. Within Mercedes Benz, as already noted, the parent company has indicated that it intends to give employee representatives in the various countries the opportunity to attend an international exchange of views on an annual basis. The real test as to whether a distinctive German-type model of a European-level information/consultation body is emerging will be the nature of any agreed arrangements developed jointly by management and employee/trade union representatives in such companies.

A strong German influence is however discernible in a recent experiment in transnational employee participation of a rather different kind - namely board-level representation - which is taking place within Europipe, a joint enterprise between the French company Usinor Sacilor and the Germany company, Mannesmann-Röhrenwerke, established on 1 January 1991. According to material relating to the formation of Europipe released by the European Commission[9], the specific legal circumstances of the company facilitated a collective agreement between management and unions which provides for parity shareholder/employee representation on the supervisory board of Europipe GmbH (six in each case) with the employee representatives being drawn from both German and French plants. The four German representatives will comprise three works council nominees and one representative from IG Metall. The two French representatives will be appointed by workers in the French factories. Although the Europipe agreement is, as far as we are aware, unique, it does represent a concrete initiative along the lines of the (German-based) employee board-level representation option contained in the European Commission's proposal for a directive on employee involvement to complement the proposed statute for a European company[10]. At the same time, the agreement also authorises the respective French and German works councils to discuss the establishment of a transnational representative body for employees.

3. EVALUATION OF PRACTICE

We turn now from the structural aspects of these European-level information and consultation forums to consider their evaluation in the eyes of those actively participating in them. We examine each of the following areas:

* origins of the initiatives;
* representation;
* operational aspects;
* benefits to management;
* benefits to employee representatives;
* negative experiences;
* future development; and
* preconditions for effectiveness.

While the arrangements in which CTS, Ford and IBC are involved do not equate to European-level information/consultation forums, interview material on their operation is nonetheless of relevance to the evaluation of practice and is accordingly incorporated here.

It should also be borne in mind that those interviewed for this Section were expressing their own opinions and that their own knowledge of structures and procedures was sometimes incomplete. In addition, the operational experience of the more recent arrangements is limited - in some cases only one or two meetings may have taken place. The analysis which follows, therefore, should be treated as tentative and provisional.

Origins of the Initiatives

The first area of investigation centred on the factors influencing management's agreeing to establishing Euro-level information/consultation arrangements.

The first three companies to do so - Thomson, Bull and BSN - were all French, and the former two nationalised (Péchiney, Rhône-Poulenc and St Gobain, later additions, were also French). The fact that the Managing Director was a Socialist was mentioned as an explicit factor at both Thomson and Bull, but also at Rhône-Poulenc (another nationalised company) where his support for legislation requiring company group-level committees (comités de groupe) within France had led him to accept its logical extension to the European-level as well. Senior management commitment was also mentioned at Nestlé where personal contacts led to initial meetings.

In all cases where an agreement had been signed, senior management had approved the arrangement (though at Bull the French human resources manager and one of the Belgian works councillors attributed its initiation to management, whilst one of the German works councillors attributed it to the EMF). At Volkswagen, the company-level works council, with support from IG-Metall and the EMF, had drawn up the draft agreement.

At Allianz and CIS the initiative came from Euro-FIET and management has been increasingly positive, partly because of the development of the single European market. In some cases, management saw information/consultation arrangements at Euro-level as a channel for company re-structuring - the closure of Videocolor in Ulm (Thomson), the acquisition of SEAT in Spain (Volkswagen) and location policy (Nestlé) were all examples in this respect. In all cases where management agreed to meetings, pressure for such a move already existed within the company, whether through the works council, national unions or European Industry Committee. However, distinctions can be drawn between those cases in which management agrees a joint formula with employee representatives and those in which it attends only at its own discretion or actually calls its own meetings (see Table 2). Management then tended to see these arrangements as a way of preempting the possibility of EC-level legislation or trade union initiatives, with Rhône-Poulenc - where management had issued invitations for 'une instance de dialogue européen' - as a striking example.

In three companies - Airbus, Gillette and Unilever - union initiatives had, on the other hand, met a steadfastly hostile reaction. In the case of Airbus, this was based partly on the view that a Euro-works council would unjustifiably lead to dual representation amongst workers seconded from its constituent European companies, whilst at Unilever management considered Euro-level worker representation to be inappropriate in a highly decentralised company structure.

We can, then, distinguish between economic, political and legal factors influencing the origin of these initiatives. Economic factors are related to the need for restructuring the company and the completion of the single European market; political factors to the state-ownership of a number of these companies and the presence of Socialist senior management; and legal factors to the prior existence of regulations on group-level enterprise committees in France, which led some companies to accept readily their extension to the European-level.

Key Points : MANAGEMENT RATIONALES

- French State-owned company
- Senior management commitment
- Prior existence of national legislation on group-level information
- Channel for facilitating company restructuring
- Response to single European market
- To pre-empt EC legislation
- To defuse trade union initiatives

Representation

Details about participation at information/consultation meetings is summarised in Table 3. The number of *management representatives* ranges from one or two (such as at Allianz and Volkswagen) up to 21 (at Nestlé). In most cases, the group's Chairman/ Managing Director and Director of Personnel and Human Resources attend, in addition to general and divisional managers from individual countries.

The number of *employee representatives*, as we noted above (p.23), ranges from 12 (BSN (Glass) and Thomson Liaison Committee) up to 75 (Elf Aquitaine), although in most cases the numbers are limited to 30 or under. The allocation of seats, country by country, is invariably determined in proportion to the number of workers employed, but political factors do intervene. At Bull, for example, there was initially a dispute over the number of seats accorded to CGT, and at Volkswagen there are two representatives for both Audi (36,000 workers) and Volkswagen Bruxelles (7000) as the two principal Belgian union confederations, FGTB and CSC, each demanded a seat. There are no formal allocations at Allianz or in respect of the sectoral arrangements to which CIS is a party as neither is a formal committee and so numbers are fairly fluid.

Nomination of employee representatives is usually carried out by the unions or works councils concerned. The Thomson Liaison Committee comprises representatives of unions affiliated to the EMF whilst its European Branch Committee is appointed by the trade unions in France, Italy, Spain and the UK (from amongst works councillors where these exist) and by the central works council in Germany or by works councils for its various divisions. Similarly, at Bull the unions make nominations, except in Austria, Germany and the Netherlands where the works councils perform this task. At Allianz and CIS nominations take place through the unions affiliated to Euro-FIET.

Problems may occasionally arise because of lack of affiliation. For example, EETPU is unable to send delegates to the IUF/Nestlé meeting despite its high density of membership in Nestlé plants, because it is not affiliated to the IUF.

In other cases, management may seek to influence nominations. St Gobain has asked the unions to be represented by works councillors, not full-time officers, whilst Rhône-

Poulenc and the EFCGU clashed on this very subject. The EFCGU had agreed that, in so far as British representation was concerned, MSF should send two members and GMB and TGWU one each to the Rhône-Poulenc meeting, but management issued invitations to the site committees at the four largest plants. As a result, MSF lost one of its representatives to a non-union employee. In addition, management is insisting on rotation of representatives which, from the unions' point of view, would hinder continuity and accountability.

In the companies investigated, there were no special provisions to ensure representation of *non-unionised employees or plants* though this issue does not arise when nominations are made through the works council (this is because all employees are represented on the European-style works council whether or not they are members of a trade union). As far as British companies are concerned, it was pointed out at CIS that since the company is fully unionised there are no non-union employees in any case.

Similarly, there were normally no special provisions to ensure representation of *white-collar or managerial staff*. Unions representing white-collar employees were often represented but in their own right. For example, the French CFE-CGC had signed the Bull agreement, and both the Belgian CNC and SETCA were involved in the meetings at St Gobain. Nor were there any special provisions, as far as we are aware, to ensure representation of any particular groups of workers such as women, part-timers, ethnic minorities or people with disabilities.

Operational Aspects

A wide variety of practice emerges when we come to analyse the operational aspects of these information/consultation arrangements - responsibility for the agenda, the holding of pre-agenda meetings, feedback of information and so on.

Responsibility for the *agenda* depends on the composition of the committee or meeting as well as on management attitudes. At Nestlé, Rhône-Poulenc and St Gobain, management makes a presentation and then invites questions so there is no formal agenda in any case. The same pattern occurred at the first meeting at Bull, although now agendas are drawn up jointly with the committee. A joint approach also prevails at Péchiney and at BSN (Food and Drink), where management collaborates with ECF/IUF, and at CIS where AECI holds joint responsibility with Euro-FIET. At Thomson, management chooses the central themes for the meetings of the Branch Committee, although union members will add points, but sets the agenda jointly with EMF for the Liaison Committee. Euro-FIET sets its own agenda for the Allianz Company Council to whose meetings it invites management.

Key Points : SETTING THE AGENDA

MANAGEMENT PRESENTATION - QUESTIONS INVITED	Nestlé, Rhône-Poulenc, St Gobain
MANAGEMENT CHOOSES CENTRAL THEMES	Thomson Branch Committee
AGENDA DRAWN UP JOINTLY	BSN (Food and Drink), Bull, CIS, Péchiney, Thomson Liaison Committee

Note: In all cases employee representatives were free to raise their own points in meetings

---

In virtually every case the employee representatives' side are in *preliminary contact* in order to decide strategy for the full meeting (national unions will themselves sometimes meet first to examine their own priorities before the international pre-meeting). In those cases where the employee representatives either do not meet management at all (such as Gillette) or do attend joint meetings on only an irregular basis (such as Ford), much of the preparation may be carried out on the telephone - otherwise, it normally takes place face to face. However, whilst the Liaison Committee at Thomson has always held preliminary meetings of this kind, the first one for the Branch Committee took place only in December 1990. The first such meeting at CIS was itself only three years ago. Whilst the unions at Allianz believe their own meetings could be better coordinated, at Bull and Volkswagen an executive committee of employee representatives prepares the groundwork.

Preliminary meetings often reveal *divergent opinions* amongst the employee representatives present. At Nestlé, for example, the UK unions had favoured women's nightwork in contrast to those of other countries which had opposed it (it was decided not to discuss the topic in the full meeting). At Bull, a German works councillor noted widely divergent interests amongst his opposite numbers - for instance, the Swiss were not concerned about unemployment though it provided a main focus for the French and Italians. At Thomson there was a wide-ranging discussion in 1989 on the position to adopt in relation to over-capacity in the audio/video business. But even leaving aside such substantive areas, the UK unions sometimes commented on divergent styles - for example, in relation to chairing meetings (Nestlé) or perception of the union's role (Allianz).

This perception of the unions' role was also a factor which sometimes led to *contrasting positions* between the employee representatives once actually in the full meeting. At Rhône-Poulenc, for example, all five French union delegations read prepared statements at the meeting in November 1990, a strategy which the German and UK unions did not understand. Otherwise, preliminary meetings usually encouraged common approaches in full meetings - at CIS disagreements had sometimes occurred before such preliminary meetings were introduced three years ago. Differences in emphasis sometimes emerged, however - at Nestlé, the German unions were particularly keen to pursue the question of location policy, whilst at Thomson the French unions were particularly concerned over the threat of job losses. The *subjects* discussed in meetings between management and employee representatives have been covered elsewhere in this report (pp.7-18) but employee representatives, who were in all cases able to raise their own points in meetings, also mentioned a variety of subjects which managements would not discuss. Sometimes these concerned national level issues which management deemed inappropriate to discuss in a European forum. Such examples occurred at Allianz when the unions attempted to broach the implementation of new technology and working conditions, and at BSN (Glass) when the unions raised the issues of pay, working time and work organisation. On one recent occasion the CFDT left the Thomson Branch Committee meeting because management, according to the union, refused to discuss the impact of its corporate strategy on employment levels.

On other occasions management eventually consented to cover subjects following initial resistance - new technology and equal opportunities at CIS, for example, which later formed the basis of jointly agreed principles of best practice, or the takeover of Honeywell and Olivetti by Bull in 1987 which Bull management, according to one of the German works councillors, would not discuss at the outset. There were also occasions, as at IBC and Nestlé, when employee representatives complained of evasive answers. So, whilst management avoids discussion in these meetings of topics relating to national levels, it should be pointed out that employee representatives were often satisfied with their open nature (for example, at BSN (Food and Drink), Rhône-Poulenc, St Gobain, the Thomson Liaison Committee and Volkswagen).

Formal minutes of meetings are kept at Allianz, Nestlé and Volkswagen and in other cases each side takes notes. These frequently serve as the basis for *feedback* of information from meetings. On the Thomson Liaison Committee, the EMF agrees minutes with management which are then written up into a report for circulation to the affiliated unions concerned. Euro-FIET produce a bulletin, *Allianz Trade Union News*, whilst ECF/IUF produce the *Nestlé Bulletin*. At CIS and IBC the unions issue circulars to all members reporting the results of their activities at European-level, whilst elsewhere national level works councils perform this function (Bull and Volkswagen, for instance). The MSF Regional Officer responsible for Allianz pointed out that while he produced newsletters for his members in Cornhill - a UK subsidiary of Allianz - since only half the workforce were unionised, the remainder would probably not receive this information. Generally, it might be assumed that feedback through works councils would be more systematic, but even there a Belgian works councillor at St Gobain complained that the employees were not interested in any issue unless it affected them directly and a French member of the Thomson Branch Committee alleged that feedback depended on the goodwill of the individual employee representative.

The use of notice boards was mentioned at BSN (Glass) and Péchiney and - perhaps surprisingly - mass meetings at BSN (Food and Drink), Gillette, Nestlé, Thomson and Volkswagen.

At Rhône-Poulenc the Chairman's presentation was being circulated to all personnel and site managers to carry out their own briefings and at St Gobain reports prepared by group management were discussed on the French group committee (comité de groupe). At Thomson, group-level management informed their local subordinates of developments because not all national managements were represented on the Liaison or Branch Committees. Minutes and tapes, produced jointly by management and the IUF, are circulated at Nestlé. At Rowntree-Mackintosh, now taken over by Nestlé, the tradition of biannual plant meetings between management and employees was being retained and - in Ireland, at least - extended to other Nestlé establishments.

Key Points : FEEDBACK OF INFORMATION

BULLETINS:

European Industry Committee	Allianz (Euro-FIET), Nestlé (ECF/IUF)
Circulars from unions	Allianz, CIS, IBC, Thomson Liaison Committee
Circulars from works councils	Bull, Volkswagen
NOTICEBOARDS	BSN (Glass), Péchiney
MASS MEETINGS	BSN (Food and Drink), Gillette, Nestlé, Thomson, Volkswagen

MANAGEMENT CIRCULARS:

To all personnel	Rhône-Poulenc
To group committee members	St Gobain

Note: This list is not exhaustive and is intended by way of illustration only

In virtually all cases, the group bears the *costs* of these meetings - the provision of facilities, travel, accommodation, meals and interpreting. The major exceptions, of course, are those where management has not yet recognised the employee representatives at Euro-level. At Gillette, costs are borne by the unions and works councils concerned, with some provision, too, through a solidarity fund, whilst at Unilever, DGV within the Commission of the EC has also supplied resources. Euro-FIET funds the Allianz Company Council, but in 1990 the company paid for the meeting at its head office in Munich.

As far as *secretarial support* for the employee representatives is concerned, the European Industry Committees play a significant role. Euro-FIET services Allianz and CIS, IUF supports BSN (Food and Drink) and Nestlé, EMF has an input into Volkswagen, and so on. At Thomson, management is responsible for secretarial aspects of the meetings or else works councils provide facilities (as at Ford). An informal employees' secretariat meets more frequently within BSN (Glass), but at Bull a union proposal for a union subcommittee to prepare meetings was turned down by management.

None of the companies investigated here had earmarked specific budgets for research or communications for these information/consultation arrangements; however, again, the European Industry Committees are key protagonists in these areas. At Unilever, for example, ECF/IUF support the research requirements of the unions involved, along with SOMO, the Dutch Centre for Research on Multinational Corporations. The economic committees of French works councils have budgets for information and coordination which may feed into some Euro-level arrangements (as at Gillette, for example).

Finally, in view of the *language* problems often encountered when developing international contacts, at least one of the unions involved - MSF - had invested time and resources in providing language training for their national and regional full-time officers.

This discussion of operational aspects is summed up in the final part of this section, 'Preconditions for Effectiveness' (p.49 below).

Benefits to Management

Management representatives were, on the whole, positive about their experiences with these information/consultation arrangements - though it should be borne in mind that they were a self-selected group: first, their companies had demonstrated a commitment to such arrangements and, second, the managers themselves had agreed to be interviewed.

The principal benefit perceived was the opportunity to exchange views and opinions both with other management colleagues and with employee representatives (mentioned at Bull, Péchiney, Rhône-Poulenc and Thomson). This was seen to encourage a fuller understanding of the group situation. Such meetings also helped to promote a sense of group identity or belonging (Rhône-Poulenc and Thomson) and, by disclosing information on corporate strategy, helped to dispel rumours about management intentions (Thomson). A manager from the former Rowntree-Mackintosh said that the meeting had assisted him, too, in understanding Nestlé's corporate plan, which shows that information disclosure is a matter not only for employee representatives but also for the management hierarchy. The suppressing of national sentiments was another benefit perceived at Thomson, whilst at Volkswagen, where the response was generally cooler, management felt that the existence of the European Group Works Council might help to promote the company's new international training programme designed to encourage greater internal mobility.

In virtually all cases, management stated that it was too early to say how these developments had improved corporate strategy. At Rhône-Poulenc, however, management was intending to refer to them in its attempts to stimulate consultation in national units where none currently took place - if consultation can take place at European-level, then why not at national level, too, ran the argument.

Similarly, it was too early to say how such developments had influenced the attitudes of employee representatives, but at Thomson management claimed that the Liaison and Branch Committees had facilitated the process of restructuring ('Four hundred redundancies in Germany and not one hour's strike' claimed the manager responsible for European social relations).

Key Points : BENEFITS TO MANAGEMENT

- Explain corporate strategy

- Facilitate company restructuring

- Foster international contacts and exchange views

- Create sense of belonging to an international company

Benefits to Employee Representatives

Overwhelmingly, employee representatives stated that Euro-level information and consultation arrangements gave them the chance to gather information direct from senior management, make new contacts with international colleagues and exchange views and best practice.

In 1990, for example, Allianz had given the MSF delegate a copy of its Report on the Business Year 1989 which had been unavailable in the UK - even through Cornhill, the Allianz subsidiary. The Report had detailed Allianz's bid to acquire Eagle Star and its strategy following German reunification. The development of international contacts made life easier for employee representatives who now actually knew their opposite numbers abroad. At Ford, these contacts had helped to resist closure of the product development centre at Cologne in 1985 - the UK unions had argued they could not handle the increased workload - and to ensure support during a strike in the UK in 1986, when the German works council had refused the transfer of work. At Unilever, the Belgian union confederation, CSC, had revealed to their UK counterparts a computer model for manpower requirements in the company whose existence had been denied by UK management. At St Gobain, employee representatives echoed the view that such international contacts made it easier to check management arguments.

Exchanges of views and best practice are also a significant benefit. The principles of best practice on new technology and equal opportunities at CIS were drawn up by collating experiences from other European countries, whilst the visit of IBC area representatives to Austria was specifically to gather information on working conditions there, particularly pensions.

Reference was also made to the fact that establishing arrangements of this kind itself set an example for other companies - BSN in relation to Nestlé, for instance - or simply to the fact that there was progress if a company was talking to the unions at this level (as in the case of Nestlé).

At Volkswagen it was felt that the European Group Works Council would promote a growing sense of international solidarity and the development of joint union strategies.

As regards the *use* made of disclosed information, most employee representatives referred to the various feedback procedures (either through the works councils or unions) outlined in an earlier section (pp.36-7). Sometimes disclosure was seen as an end in itself since there was not always an immediate use for information. But the unions also used it in a number of cases in domestic collective bargaining - the comparison of conditions in other European countries was a resource in negotiating improved terms at home (at BSN (Food and Drink), CIS and IBC, for instance).

There were only a few examples of unions developing joint policies on the areas covered by these information/consultation arrangements. Whilst exchange of information had improved between the unions themselves, problems of language, difficulties in comparing legal frameworks and working conditions and divergent union and political attitudes were sometimes cited as hindrances to this kind of joint development (for example, at Allianz and St Gobain). Coordination took place principally over the issues raised in full meetings, but a number of employee representatives stressed their wish to see the evolution of joint policies (at BSN (Food and Drink), BSN (Glass), Bull and Nestlé, for example). Whilst a member of the Thomson Branch Committee felt that there was still too much competition between subsidiaries in this respect, the EMF Thomson working party is engaged on the formulation of joint policy for Thomson (and influence is, therefore, exerted indirectly through EMF).

The question of competition between subsidiaries was also raised at Gillette where divergent attitudes amongst the unions over Sunday working and nightwork impeded fuller cooperation, though at Volkswagen joint policies had been hammered out, including rejection of weekend work and a 35-hour week by 1993. Even here, however, works councillors were conscious of divergences in relation to nightwork.

In a number of cases, employee representatives felt that they had influenced management attitudes or policy through these meetings. In several instances representatives claimed that management now had to take the arrangements into account in formulating their own policies, for example at Bull, Ford, Thomson and Volkswagen. At BSN (Food and Drink) one of the German works councillors, a member of the foodworkers' union, NGG, claimed that employment in biscuit production had been safeguarded following management's positive reactions to union proposals made at one of the Euro-level meetings, whilst at Bull management had agreed to the addition of employee representatives from Italy and the UK in 1989 - outside the terms of the 1988 agreement setting up the original committee - owing to union pressure. At Thomson, it was felt that methods of restructuring would now be more careful because of the existence of the committees; and at Volkswagen, according to a Belgian works councillor, a member of FGTB, management in Belgium had to give up subcontracting production of seats for the Golf car to a textile factory where wage rates were below those in the automobile industry and retain the jobs of over 500 women within Volkswagen following coordinated action by the Belgian and German unions. Management at SEAT also allegedly gave up plans to introduce Saturday shift-working in Spain following pressure exerted through the European Group Works Council. In addition, the existence of these links had helped dispel the fear that management would 'play off' one subsidiary against another. Whilst it was often acknowledged that this could still occur, even between plants in a single country, a Euro-level committee structure would help prevent this (BSN (Food and Drink), Bull, Gillette, St Gobain, Thomson and Volkswagen).

Overall, then, the principal benefits of these arrangements as perceived by employee representatives included the chance to gather information direct from group headquarters, the use of information for domestic collective bargaining purposes and the gradual formulation of joint policies with other unions at a European level.

Key Points : BENEFITS TO EMPLOYEE REPRESENTATIVES

- Gather information direct from group headquarters
- Use information for national collective bargaining
- Improve international contacts
- Exchange information on best practice
- Set example for other multinationals
- Develop joint international policy

Negative Experiences

As regards management, very few negative experiences were registered. The political nature of the French trade unions (Rhône-Poulenc) and the difficulty of maintaining interest in the Euro-level committees in non-crisis situations (Thomson) were the only two mentioned.

As regards employee representatives, too, there were on the whole not many negative experiences although, as the CFDT representative at BSN (Glass) pointed out, these arrangements are still very recent. However, one meeting per year was sometimes seen as insufficient to allow the monitoring of points raised, for example developments in a company's acquisition policy. At IBC the unions had been outnumbered on their Austrian visit by management, so management issues had predominated. In some cases management set the agenda for meetings and, at Rhône-Poulenc, had selected the employee representatives who could attend, stipulating that they wanted their rotation on an annual basis. The unions feared that this would lead to lack of accountability and incorporation into management procedures and that they would be unable to call a meeting themselves in an emergency. Problems arose, as we saw in an earlier section (p.42) over divergent policies in relation to, for example, Sunday working and nightwork at Gillette, with the Germans against, the Spanish in favour and the French accepting it in order to keep jobs. At Ford, inter-union problems of this kind had not arisen - perhaps because the unions have had such a strong influence over the initiatives to establish joint visits in the first place, often through the relevant European Industry Committee.

Union structures themselves also presented problems in other ways. The UK electricians' unions, EETPU, for example, is not affiliated to the IUF which had campaigned for information and consultation arrangements at Nestlé, and so was not represented at the first meeting even though it is a major union within the company's UK plants. There were also sometimes divergent approaches amongst the unions, with the UK unions adopting a pragmatic approach to the meetings in contrast to the French unions' more ideological approach. Overall, the most negative views were expressed by the French trade unionists, perhaps for this reason.

Problems of interpreting and translation were also mentioned, especially amongst the UK unions - it was not always clear, for example, just how senior, in fact, managers were from their job titles, and language difficulties led to a formality which hampered free discussion. Sometimes debate was also hindered by lack of awareness of foreign institutions - at Allianz, for instance, the concept of performance-related pay had to be explained to the Italian unions.

> **Key Points : NEGATIVE EXPERIENCES - UNIONS**
>
> - Only one meeting per year
> - Little follow-up
> - Divergent aims amongst unions
> - Management sets agenda
> - Management chooses employee representatives
> - Lack of accountability
> - Translation/interpreting problems

Future Development

In all cases managements believed that the unions wished to extend their involvement at European level, particularly by transforming information disclosure into consultation. At Thomson, IG-Metall and CFDT were perceived as the prime movers in this direction, whilst management at Rhône-Poulenc stated firmly that any such attempts 'will be resisted' since national level consultation/negotiation already existed and there was no need for further developments at European level. At Volkswagen, on the other hand, the unions were not yet seen by management as ready for greater influence.

The employee representatives themselves expressed a wider range of views over future involvement. At Airbus, Allianz, Gillette, Unilever and Volkswagen they wanted recognition first and foremost, although at both Allianz and Volkswagen they were aware that management had come under pressure from other companies in their respective sectors *not* to sign in order to avoid establishing a precedent for the unions to use elsewhere. At Nestlé there was a desire on the part of the employee representatives to use the annual meetings as a basis to establish a formal European works council. At Ford, too, steps were being taken to secure a European works council for Ford Europe: the Belgian, French and Spanish unions had already forged close links and IG-Metall had drawn up a draft constitution for which consent was being sought, particularly in the UK where at least one major union was thought to have reservations.

Otherwise the unions advocated the development of consultation and collective bargaining from existing provisions for information disclosure - a point made at BSN (Food and Drink) and BSN (Glass), Bull, Thomson and Volkswagen - as well as an extension in the subjects to be covered at meetings. At CIS, the unions wanted statements of best practice on annual holidays; at Nestlé, an agreement on equal opportunities; and at Thomson, a wider remit to cover other European-level issues like health and safety, working time and pensions (though not pay). At Thomson there was a call for arbitration procedures in cases of conflict and the right to summon external experts if need be, a call echoed at Volkswagen where the provision of more timely information was also urged.

Key Points : FUTURE DEVELOPMENT

Management objectives:

- Maintain existing arrangements
- Improve channels of communication

Union objectives:

- Formalise informal arrangements
- Develop European-level consultation
- Develop European-level negotiation
- Extend the number of multinationals with information/consultation arrangements

Employee representatives were uncertain over how management wanted these information/consultation arrangements to develop. At BSN (Glass) and Nestlé it was felt that the arrangements had been established too recently to tell, whilst at BSN (Food and Drink) the goodwill which had now been generated could lead - it was suggested - to consultation, not as a formal right but *de facto*. At Bull, management agreed with the employee representatives that the competence of the committee should be extended if serious problems, for example over restructuring plans, were to be solved. Management at St Gobain was thought - correctly - to be content with the current system but the CFDT representative on the Thomson Branch Committee maintained that much depended on the personality of the Managing Director.

Generally speaking, managements favoured improved channels of communication but did not want greater formality or an extension of powers as far as existing arrangements were concerned. Only at Bull was a preference expressed for moves in such a direction and then towards consultation rather than negotiation. Employee representatives were well aware that managements generally feared an encroachment of their powers at this level.

Employee representatives generally expressed a positive attitude towards the role of the Commission of the EC in promoting participation - particularly at Nestlé, where details of the current arrangement were worked out jointly with ECF/IUF and DGV, and Unilever, where the Commission has materially supported the unions' campaign for Euro-level talks with management. At Allianz, the unions felt that the European Works Council directive would endorse recognition of the Company Council. Similarly, at Volkswagen, the directive was seen as the springboard for the proliferation of European works councils (although the caveat was added at Bull that unions would nevertheless be responsible for triggering the procedures envisaged by the directive).

However, amongst the employee representatives we interviewed, EC legislation was not always considered vital in promoting these developments (Ford, Nestlé, St Gobain and Thomson). At Bull, for example, one of the German works councillors claimed that feedback from unions in other sectors could do much to promote best practice, but added that it was difficult to keep track of developments in this area as so little information was available.

By way of contrast, managements at Nestlé, Péchiney and Thomson declared that the prospect of EC legislation had been a major influence in setting up appropriate information/consultation arrangements.

Both management - especially at Péchiney, Rhône-Poulenc and Thomson - and employee representatives stressed the importance of voluntary arrangements in this area, particularly as role models for other companies. This view was expressed at Bull, Gillette, St Gobain, Thomson and Volkswagen, with the unions at CIS and Ford adding that all progress in their cases had been on a voluntary basis. Naturally, for this very reason, these responses were from a self-selected sample. By contrast, at Allianz and Unilever where there is no management recognition of Euro-level procedures, the unions stressed that the European Works Council directive would bring positive benefits. At Nestlé one of the German works councillors said that it all came down to quantity: the more voluntary agreements there were, the greater their influence, but the problem was that because there were, in fact, so few they had very little influence - so a legislative approach was required instead.

Key Points : ATTITUDES TOWARDS VOLUNTARY AGREEMENTS

Agreements must be voluntary -

- Compulsion damages flexibility
- Practice creates basis for subsequent legislation

Legislation is essential -

- Failure of voluntarist approach
- Comprehensive coverage is required
- Necessary to ensure fair application

Preconditions for Effectiveness

Overall, the managers we interviewed, as we saw above (p.39), expressed general satisfaction with existing arrangements and did not advocate major changes (though management at Rhône-Poulenc hoped to improve communications within the framework of the Euro-level meetings they intended to hold annually). However, from the unions' point of view, a number of preconditions for the effective operation of these arrangements emerged.

A jointly formulated agenda allowed employee representatives greater scope, they felt, for steering discussion. Research and secretarial support, which was most notably forthcoming in those cases where initiatives had been promoted by one of the European Industry Committees, like EMF or Euro-FIET, was clearly important if employee representatives were to be properly briefed beforehand. Similarly, preparatory meetings allowed the unions to coordinate their questioning, though some unions complained of difficulties in organising - and paying for - such preparation given the number of unions and countries involved. Joint strategy for the *use* of information disclosed rarely emerged; where it did, it had been elaborated through one of the European Industry Committees. Otherwise, unions used the information principally in their own domestic bargaining strategies.

A variety of channels existed for the feedback of information into the union structures: bulletins, newsletters and reports were all mentioned, circulated either through the unions or works councils. At Rhône-Poulenc, the Chairman's presentation was circulated to all site managers for team briefings. The effectiveness of this feedback depended on the links between the employee representatives and the appropriate structures - where they were isolated, little flow of information could be expected.

Language training also featured as an item for success, or at least professional interpreting/translating facilities. In one case, a discussion between a UK union official and German manager was disrupted because the interpreter - himself a manager - began to take sides and argue back!

Key Points : UNION PRECONDITIONS FOR EFFECTIVENESS

- Jointly drawn up agendas

- Preparatory meetings

- Strategy for use of information

- Channels to feed back information

- Employee representatives linked into union structures

- Research and secretarial support

- Language training

4. THE DRAFT EUROPEAN WORKS COUNCILS DIRECTIVE

In drawing up its proposals for the European Works Councils directive, the Commission sought the views of management and employee representatives party to certain of these arrangements[11], and the directive's minimum requirements for the constitution of European Works Councils reflect to a significant extent the pattern established by existing European-level information and consultation bodies[12].

The essential requirement of the proposed directive is the establishment of a European Works Council (or similar arrangement) in every 'Community-scale' undertaking or group of undertakings where this is requested by employees or their representatives (or, indeed, initiated by central management). In the amended proposal for the directive, adopted by the Commission in September 1991, 'Community-scale undertaking' is defined as an undertaking with at least 1000 employees within the Community, including at least 100 employees in each of two or more member states. Similarly, a 'Community-scale group of undertakings' is a group with at least 1000 employees within the Community and with at least two group undertakings in different member states, each employing at least 100 employees within the Community.

It is intended that the scope, composition, competence and mode of operation of European Works Councils should be a matter for agreement between the management of the undertaking or group and a 'special negotiating body' of existing employee representatives. Indeed, it is open to the special negotiating body to agree - unanimously - not to seek the establishment of a European Works Council. Where the special negotiating body does decide to enter into discussions with management, but agreement is not reached after a year, certain minimum requirements (to be laid down by member states in accordance with the directive) are to apply. The directive also enables the special negotiating body and the undertaking or group management to agree not to establish a European Works Council but to operate alternative information and consultation arrangements which otherwise meet these minimum requirements.

The minimum requirements set out in the amended proposal for the directive provide that the competence of European Works Councils will be limited to those matters which concern the undertaking or group as a whole or those which concern two or more establishments or group undertakings located in different member states. On this basis, European Works Councils will have the right to meet central management annually to be *informed* of the undertaking or group's progress and prospects. They will also have the right to be *consulted* on management proposals 'likely to have serious consequences for the interests of the employees' (including mergers/closures/relocations, organisational change, and new working or production methods), for which purpose European Works Councils may request one additional meeting a year with management, if necessary. The minimum requirements also provide that European Works Councils will have a maximum of 30 members drawn from existing employee representatives, or specially elected where there are no employee representatives. The operating expenses of European Works Councils are to be met by the undertaking or group concerned.

There is thus a broad correlation between the minimum requirements set out in the directive and current practice in the multinationals examined in Section 2, but with certain important exceptions. First, by envisaging a formal (if limited) consultative procedure involving European Works Councils, the directive goes beyond the information-only remit typical of most existing European-level bodies. It provides for consultation on any management proposal (of transnational applicability) 'likely to have serious consequences for the interests of the employees ... on the basis of a report from the central management ... on which the European Works Council may put forward its opinion. The final decision shall be exclusively the responsibility of the central management'. French legislation, by comparison, does not give national group enterprise committees consultative powers, whereas German group works councils are authorised to deal - on the basis of the works council rights laid down in the 1972 Works Constitution Act - with matters which concern the group or two or more group undertakings, but only where such matters cannot be settled by individual central (undertaking-level) works councils or are delegated to it by a central works council. In the Netherlands, too, group-wide works councils may assume formal consultative powers under the 1971 Works Councils Act in relation to matters of common interest to all or most of the undertakings they cover.

The second major exception to the basic model established by existing arrangements is the fact that the directive provides no formal role for 'external' trade union organisations - whether national or European-level - in the European Works Council procedure. The directive, in effect, leaves the matter to member states' legislation. The special negotiating body and the European Works Council (at least where the minimum requirements apply) are to be made up of representatives of the employees of the undertaking or group in question, with special arrangements where there are no employee representatives. 'Representatives of the employees' are defined as 'employees' representatives provided for by the laws or practice of the member states'. Thus it is intended that, for example, representatives of recognised *trade unions* from plants or undertakings in Britain and Ireland - perhaps including full-time officials - would co-exist with *works council* members from, say, France, Germany and the Netherlands within the European Works Council structure.

Moreover, the *method* by which representatives of the employees (or, in their absence, the body of employees) should appoint or elect the members of either the special negotiating body or the European Works Council is to be determined by each member state. In France, Germany and the Netherlands, there are already established systems for the nomination of representatives to national group level works councils. In Germany and the Netherlands, this is by election or appointment from lower-tier works councils. In France, group enterprise committee members are appointed proportionally by the representative unions from among their elected enterprise committee members - a system reflected in the arrangements for European-level information and consultation bodies in the French multinationals discussed above - or, if non-union lists predominate in enterprise committees, by the departmental Director of Labour.

A further point is that, under the directive, European Works Councils consist entirely of employee representatives (as for example in Germany): they do not take the form of joint management/employee bodies as under the French pattern. The practical significance of this, though, is limited. The minimum requirements define the role of European Works Councils almost exclusively in terms of meetings with management, their only entitlement to meet separately being prior to meetings with management.

The Views of the Social Partners

The responses of the ETUC and UNICE to the proposed European Works Councils directive reflect starkly differing approaches. The ETUC has welcomed the Commission's proposal while identifying certain improvements it wishes to see (in terms of lower workforce size thresholds and stronger consultation rights). The ETUC's response states that 'the completion of the internal market encourages the centralisation of corporate decision-making processes at European level. There is, therefore, a pressing need for a Community-level guaranteed right for workers and their representatives to be informed and consulted'[13]. The ETUC also welcomes the directive's policy of leaving the constitution of the European Works Council to negotiation, at least in the first instance. Following a conference on European Works Councils in Maastricht in September 1991, the ETUC is coordinating a campaign to maximise the number of European-level information and consultation bodies established within multinational companies[14].

UNICE, on the other hand, finds the proposed directive 'totally unacceptable'. UNICE emphasises that companies have evolved a variety of information and consultation procedures to suit their particular circumstances, and that a single legislative approach is inflexible and harmful. It is also argued that the directive's requirements are incompatible with decentralised management structures, and that in any case consultation is most appropriately carried out at the level of the workplace, that is, with the workers directly affected by a particular decision[15]. In October 1991, UNICE issued proposals for a (non-binding) Recommendation by the EC Council of Ministers on information and consultation procedures, under which local management would be responsible for the provision of all relevant information - obtained if necessary from their parent company - and for consulting employees or their representatives[16].

5. SUMMARY AND CONCLUSION

This report has identified and analysed the European-level information and consultation arrangements currently operating in eleven major European multinational companies. As we saw in Table 2, the arrangements in three of the companies are based on formal written agreements and in three other companies constitute an agreed practice. In the remainder of the companies investigated, informal arrangements operate - in two cases initiated by management, in three cases by employee representatives but with informal management cooperation. In these latter three cases such a cautious management approach should not perhaps be surprising. After all, many other multinationals are strongly resistant to any form of European-level information and consultation. But a willingness informally to sanction the operation of such arrangements without committing the group irretrievably to a particular package may also be a reflection of management's concern to await the outcome of current legislative moves within the EC.

The most striking feature of the companies concerned is that French based multinationals predominate. Indeed, it has been possible to identify a set of key characteristics or a basic model with which each of the existing jointly agreed European-level information and consultation arrangements investigated is broadly consistent. This basic model appears to be influenced to a significant extent by French legislation, introduced in 1982, governing the establishment of *national* group-level enterprise committees. So, for example, the jointly agreed European-level information and consultation procedures in the multinationals investigated tend to be relatively small joint management/employee bodies which meet annually for the purpose of discussing company information provided by management, and whose employee members are nominated by appropriate trade unions from among existing works councillors within the company.

A variant of this basic model is the informal arrangements at the German-based multinationals - Allianz, Mercedes Benz and Volkswagen - where employee/trade union-initiated councils are accorded a degree of informal recognition and cooperation by management, though in each case the trade unions/employee representatives concerned are actively seeking the establishment of a formal joint European-level information/ consultation body. A more clear-cut - but isolated - example of the influence of

The employee representatives comprise one national trade union officer from each of the countries in which the group operates, plus delegates from Nestlé plants nominated by ECF/IUF unions, whose members reflect the distribution of the Nestlé workforce in each country concerned. A maximum of 50 employee representatives participate. Senior management representatives from Nestlé Europe and its national subsidiaries also attend. The next meeting is scheduled for autumn 1991. Delegates who are Nestlé employees receive paid time off to participate in the meetings and the expenses of all participants are met by Nestlé. The purpose of the meeting is confined to the provision and discussion of company information.

Elf Aquitaine

In July 1991, Elf Aquitaine signed an agreement with a number of union organisations at national and European level establishing a European Information and Concertation Body (une instance européene d'information et de concertation) with a view to promoting 'a constructive social dialogue' within the group at European level (that is, covering Elf Aquitaine subsidiaries in the EC and EFTA). The body is to consider 'economic, financial and social issues' including the group's organisation and operations, corporate strategy, annual budgets and balance sheets, and employment policy. The agreement states that 'the role of the body will be to supplement the work of similar national bodies' and that 'under no circumstances may it substitute for them or impair the rights of employees and their representatives in each country'.

The body will meet once a year, though if circumstances require it, another extraordinary meeting may be called in the same year. There is also a provision envisaging the eventual development of similar yearly meetings within individual divisions of the group. The plenary meeting will be preceded each day by preparatory meetings, for which the required facilities will be made available by the group. Travel and accommodation costs and expenses for time spent in connection with the body will be borne by the Elf subsidiary to which each representative belongs. The agreement will operate for a two-year trial period, at the end of which conditions for renewal and future running of the body will be reviewed.

multinational corporation's ability to take advantage of different labour market conditions in different countries, then companies can be expected to resist their establishment. Indeed, a key aspect of many multinationals' resistance to these forums is likely to be the fear that the establishment of representative institutions at European level may provide a platform from which trade unions may seek to develop European-level *collective bargaining* in the context of Community moves towards economic and monetary union[17].

The development of European-level collective bargaining is something to which the management respondents in our survey were implacably opposed. At the same time, however, as Section 3 of the report has shown, the companies they represent have in a number of cases agreed to or even initiated the establishment of European-level information and consultation bodies to facilitate the implementation of company restructuring plans. Some other companies have seen the introduction of limited European-level information and consultation arrangements as a means of heading off EC legislative moves or more ambitious trade union objectives.

Further factors influencing management policy are suggested in another recent analysis by Paul Marginson[18] which focuses on whether some types of company may be more likely to opt for European-level information and consultation arrangements than others. He argues that the companies developing a European-wide approach to employment and industrial relations matters, either at group or business division level, are most likely to be those with a single ownership structure, whose management is organised around international business divisions, and where they produce similar products and services in different countries or integrate production across national boundaries. On this basis, as companies reorganise themselves in the run-up to the completion of the single European market and beyond, the number of European-level information and consultation arrangements can be expected to continue to increase.

Whether the European Works Councils directive is eventually passed, or whether the spread of European-level information and consultation arrangements continues to depend on voluntary means, the innovative transnational industrial relations procedures which have been the central focus of this report will provide a key reference point for employers, trade unions and European policy-makers alike.

Key Points : CONCLUSIONS

- Small number of European - level information/consultation bodies so far, but spreading

- Such bodies share common characteristics

- Outside such bodies a wide variety of other arrangements exists - many are informal, not formal

- Most arrangements provide only information: there is little consultation and no negotiation

- Existing arrangements have influenced the European Works Councils directive

- Platform for development of European-level collective bargaining?

REFERENCES

1. Gunnar Myrvang Information and Consultation Rights in the Nordic Countries : Experiences and Perspectives, Nordic Foundation for Industrial Development : Copenhagen (1991)

2. BSN et le syndicalisme international: Bilan de la situation au 1er juin 1990, Groupe BSN (September 1990) annex 2.

3. Création d'un comité européen de consultation BSN, ECF/IUF Press Release : Brussels (30 October 1986).

4. BSN et le syndicalisme international: Bilan de la situation au 1er juin 1990, Groupe BSN (September 1990) annex 6.

5. Press release - European Employee Representative Committee, Mercedes Benz, Utrecht (March 1991).

6. Michael Gold and Mark Hall, Legal Regulation and the Practice of Employee Participation in the European Community, European Foundation for the Improvement of Living and Working Conditions, Working Paper No. EF/WP/90/41/EN. Dublin (1990) p.14.

7. Herbert R Northrup, Duncan C Campbell and Betty J Slowinski 'Multinational union-management consultation in Europe: Resurgence in the 1980s?', International Labour Review, vol.127, No.5 (1988) p.534.

    See also : Dirk Buda and Jean Vogel, L'Europe Sociale 1992 : Illusion, Alibi ou Realité, rapport no. 2, L'Institut de Sociologie de l'Université Libre de Bruxelles, Brussels (June 1989) p.17, footnote 1.

8. European Metalworkers' Federation, EMF Position Paper on Workers' Information Rights in Multinational Companies, Brussels (July 1988).

9. Dienst des Sprechers (Spokesman's Service) 'Die Kommission genehmigt die Gründung eines gemeinsamen Unternehmens Europipe SA durch Usinor Sacilor SA und Mannesmann-Röhrenwerke AG', Commission of the EC Press Release, Brussels (7 January 1991).

10. Proposal for a Council Regulation on the Statute for a European Company and proposal for a Council Directive complementing the Statute for a European Company with regard to the involvement of employees in the European Company, Commission of the EC, COM (89) 268 Final, Brussels (25 August 1989).

11. Proposal for a Council Directive on the establishment of a European Works Council in Community-scale undertakings or groups of undertakings for the purposes of informing and consulting employees, Commission of the EC, COM (90) 581 Final, Brussels (25 January 1991).
    Amended Proposal, Commission of the EC, COM (91) 345 Final, Brussels (adopted by the Commission September 1991).

12. Mark Hall, 'Employee Participation and the European Community: the Evolution of the European Works Councils Directive' Paper for the International Industrial Relations Association European Regional Congress, Bari (23-25 September 1991) p.11.

13. ETUC Executive Committee Declaration on proposed European Works Council Directive, Brussels (15 February 1991).

14. The European Works Council is on its Way, ETUC Executive Committee Resolution, Brussels (31 October 1991).

15. UNICE Position Paper on proposed European Works Council Directive, Brussels (4 March 1991).

16. UNICE's Approach to Community Action with regard to Information and Consultation, Brussels (7 October 1991).

17. Peter Coldrick, 'Collective Bargaining in the New Europe', Personnel Management (October 1990).

18. Paul Marginson, 'Bargaining in ECUs? European Integration and Transnational Management-Union Relations in the Enterprise' Paper for the International Industrial Relations Association European Regional Congress, Bari (23-25 September 1991).

SELECT BIBLIOGRAPHY

English

Amended Proposal for a Council directive on the establishment of a European Works Council in Community-scale undertakings or groups of undertakings for the purposes of informing and consulting employees, Commission of the EC, COM (91) 345 Final, Brussels (adopted by the Commission September 1991).

Coldrick, Peter   'Collective Bargaining in the new Europe', Personnel Management (October 1990).

European Trade Union Institute, The Social Dimension of the Internal Market. Second Part: Workers' Rights in European Companies, Info 26, Brussels (1988).

European Trade Union Institute, Agreements on Workers' Information and Consultation Rights in European Multinationals and an Evaluation of Experience, Brussels (September 1991).

Hall, Mark   'Employee Participation and the European Community : the Evolution of the European Works Council Directive' Paper for the International Industrial Relations Association European Regional Congress, Bari (23-25 September 1991).

International Labour Office, Multinational Enterprises and Social Policy, Geneva (1973).

International Labour Office, Relations between Management of Transnational Enterprises and Employee Representatives in Certain Countries of the EC, International Institute for Labour Studies Research Series No. 51, Geneva (1979).

Marginson, Paul   'Bargaining in ECUs? European Integration and Transnational Management-Union Relations in the Enterprise' Paper for the International Industrial Relations Association European Regional Congress, Bari (23-25 September 1991).

Marginson, Paul, and Mark Hall, 'European-level Management-Union Relations in Transnational Enterprises' Research Review, Industrial Relations Research Unit, University of Warwick, No.4 (August 1991).

Myrvang, Gunnar   Information and Consultation Rights in Transnational Companies : the Nordic Experience European Foundation for the Improvement of Living and Working Conditions, Working Paper No. EF/WP/90/29/EN, Dublin (1990).

Myrvang, Gunnar   Information and Consultation Rights in the Nordic Countries : Experiences and Perspectives Nordic Foundation for Industrial Development, Copenhagen (1991).

Proposal for a Council directive on the establishment of a European Works Council in Community-scale undertakings or groups of undertakings for the purposes of informing and consulting employees, Commission of the EC, COM (90) 581 Final, Brussels (25 January 1991).

O'Kelly, Kevin   'The Future of Employee Relations within European Enterprises' Paper for a conference on Work, Employment and European Society : Convergence and Integration, University of Bath (6-8 September 1990) (Reproduced by the European Foundation for the Improvement of Living and Working Conditions, Dublin (1990)).

Northrup, Herbert R., Duncan C Campbell and Betty J Slowinski   'Multinational Union-Management Consultation in Europe : Resurgence in the 1980s?' International Labour Review, vol. 127, no. 5 (1988).

French

Buda, Dirk and Jean Vogel L'Europe Sociale 1992 : Illusion, Alibi ou Réalité, rapport no. 2, L'Institut de Sociologie de l'Université Libre de Bruxelles, Brussels (June 1989).

'Conseil de groupe européen chez Volkswagen: enjeux représentatifs et syndicaux', IRES Chronique Internationale, No. 9 (March 1991).

Jobert, Annette 'La négociation collective dans les entreprises multinationales en Europe' in G. Devin (ed.) Syndicalisme : dimensions internationales, editions européennes ERASME, Paris (1990).

German

Buda, Dirk Auf dem Weg zum europäischen Betriebsrat, Friedrich Ebert Stiftung, Bonn : Reihe Eurokolleg 6 (1991).

'Die Uhr läuft : Mitbestimmung und Demokratie - Fremdwörter in Europa?' Der Gewerkschafter, no. 12 (1990).

Mitbestimmung no. 4 (1991) :

- 'Ein gemeinsamer gewerkschaftlicher Weg gegen die Standortkonkurrenz'

- 'Arbeitnehmertreffs quer durch Europa unterstützen die nationale Interessenvertretung', Dirk Buda.

- 'Erste Schritte zur Europäisierung der Interessenvertretung in der chemischen Industrie', Rolf Jäger.

- 'Skandinavien : Länderübergreifende Belegschaftsinformation verleiht Stärke', Gunnar Myrvang.

'Politisches Neuland', WirtschaftsWoche, no. 23 (31 May 1991).

ABBREVIATIONS

AECI	Association of European Cooperative Insurers
CFDT	Confédération Française Democratique du Travail
CFE-CGC	Confédération Française de l'Encadrement
CFTC	Confédération Française des Travailleurs Chrétiens
CGT	Confédération Generale du Travail
CIS	Cooperative Insurance Society
CNC	Confédération Nationale des Cadres
CNT	Confederación Nacional del Trabajo
CSC	Confédération des Syndicats Chrétiens de Belgique
DGV	Directorate-General for Employment, Industrial Relations and Social Affairs of the Commission of the EC
EC	European Communities
ECF/IUF	European Committee of Food, Catering and Allied Workers' Unions within the IUF
EETPU	Electrical Electronic Telecommunications and Plumbing Union
EFCGU	European Federation of Chemical and General Workers' Unions
EFTA	European Free Trade Association
EMF	European Metalworkers' Federation in the Community
ETUC	European Trade Union Confederation
Euro-FIET	European Regional Organisation of FIET
FGTB	Fédération Générale du Travail de Belgique
FIET	International Federation of Commercial, Clerical and Technical Employees
FO	Force-Ouvrière
GMB	General Municipal Boilermakers and Allied Trades Union
IG Metall	Industriegewerkschaft Metall (German Metalworkers' Union)
IUF	International Union of Food and Allied Workers' Associations
MD	Managing Director
MNC	Multinational Corporation
MSF	Manufacturing Science Finance Union
NGG	Gewerkshaft Nahrung-Gaststätten-Genuss (German food and drink, hotels and catering union)
SETCA	Syndicat d'Employés, Techniciens et Cadres
SOMO	Stichting Onderzoek Multinationale Ondernemingen (Centre for Research on Multinational Corporations)
TGWU	Transport and General Workers' Union
UNICE	Union of Industrial and Employers' Confederations of Europe

APPENDIX I : Company Profiles

NAME OF COMPANY	NATIONALITY	SECTOR	APPROXIMATE NUMBERS EMPLOYED
Airbus Industrie	Partnership of four European aerospace companies: Aérospatiale (French) 37.9%; Deutsche Airbus (German) 37.9%; British Aerospace (British) 20%; Casa (Spain) 4.2%.	Aerospace	1200, of whom about half are recruited directly and the rest seconded from the partner companies (250 Aérospatiale, 250 Deutsche Airbus, 80 British Aerospace, 20 Casa).
Allianz	German	Financial services	55,000 across Europe, with 25,000 in Germany.
BSN-Group	French	1) Food and Drink Division	63,000 worldwide
		2) Glass Division	8590 with 5670 in France, 1810 in the Netherlands and 1110 in Spain.
Bull Group	French	Information technology	22,000 in Europe, with 17,000 in France
Cooperative Insurance Society	British	Financial services	74,700 are employed in the cooperative insurance sector across six European countries.
Ford	U S	Motor manufacture (product development)	100,000 in Ford Europe, with 2000 and 3000 respectively in the Cologne and Dunton product development centres.
Gillette	U S	Surgical and personal hygiene	3200 in Europe, with 1300 in Germany, 1000 in the UK, 400 in France, 300 in Spain and 200 in Italy.

NAME OF COMPANY	NATIONALITY	SECTOR	APPROXIMATE NUMBERS EMPLOYED
IBC Vehicles	UK-based joint venture: General Motors (US) and Isuzu (Japan)	Motor manufacture (vans)	1750 in UK.
Nestlé	Swiss	Food and drink	85,000 across 17 European countries, with 26,000 in the UK and 16,000 in Germany.
Péchiney	French	Primary aluminium production	41,500 with 30,500 in France, and the rest across seven other EC member states.
Rhône-Poulenc	French	Chemicals / agro-chemicals	92,000 worldwide, with 41,200 in France, and 17,500 across the rest of Europe.
St Gobain	French	Glass container manufacture	105,000 worldwide, with 65,000 in Europe (40,000 in France and 1200 in Belgium).
Thomson Consumer Electronics	French	Information technology	16,800 in Europe, with 5700 in France, 5600 in Germany, 2500 in Italy, 1700 in the UK and 1300 in Spain.
Unilever	Anglo/Dutch	Food, chemicals	110,000 in Europe, with 40,000 in the UK, 24,000 in Germany, 13,000 in the Netherlands, 10,000 in France and 5000 in Belgium. The rest are spread across seven other European countries.
Volkswagen	German	Motor manufacture	Almost 200,000 in Europe, with 128,000 at Volkswagen and 36,000 at Audi in Germany, 25,000 at SEAT in Spain and 7000 at Volkswagen Bruxelles in Belgium.

APPENDIX II : Key Documents

Agreements :	Bull	
	Thomson	- Liaison Committee
		- European Branch Committee
	Elf Aquitaine	
Exchange of Letters :	BSN / IUF	- Food and Drink
	BSN/CGT and CNT	- Glass
Common Viewpoint :	BSN / IUF	- Food and Drink
Model Draft Agreements:	EMF	
	FIET	

(March 1988)

AGREEMENT

**CONCERNING THE SETTING-UP OF THE
BULL EUROPEAN INFORMATION COMMITTEE**

Between the General Management of the BULL Group and the representative trade union organisations indicated below:-

C.F.E. - C.G.C.

C.F.D.T.

C.F.T.C.

C.G.T.

C.G.T. - F.O.

ARTICLE 1

It has been deemed advisable to set up a European information and consultation body for the purpose of establishing a dialogue in the European countries in which BULL is located. This body will be called the "Bull European Information Committee".

The Committee thus formed shall be made up of a total of 23 shopstewards/lay representatives broken down as follows:-

France	:	BULL SA	10
		BULL CP 8	1
Germany	:	BULL AG	2
Netherlands	:	BULL NEDERLAND NV	1
Austria	:	BULL AG	1
Belgium	:	NV BULL SA	1
Denmark	:	BULL A/S	1
Spain	:	BULL (ESPANA) SA	1
Greece	:	BULL AE	1
Norway	:	BULL A/S	1
Portugal	:	BULL PORTUGUESA COMPUTADORES Lda	1
Sweden	:	BULL AB	1
Switzerland	:	BULL (SCHWEIZ) AG	1

The appointment of representatives shall be subject to negotiations in each of the countries concerned. These negotiations will take into account current legislation in each of the countries concerned and will give rise to the signature of an additional clause to the agreement signed by the management of each company and the trade union representatives or failing this staff representatives.

To facilitate understanding of the information provided at meetings, proceedings will be in French and English.

The meetings, of which there will be two during the lifetime of the agreement, will take place during the third quarter of 1988 and the second quarter of 1989, respectively.

The Group Management will meet the travel and accommodation costs incurred by the lay representatives/ shopstewards in respect of the two plenary meetings plus the preparatory meeting, in accordance with the regulations concerning travel expenses in force in the countries concerned. If other needs arise, these will be subject to negotiation between the signatories.

Participants will be informed of the venue of the meeting and meeting arrangements eight weeks prior to the date of the meeting and will thus have the opportunity to organise a preparatory meeting in the intervening period.

The information supplied at these meetings will relate to trading, economic, financial and social matters in respect of the whole of the Group. This information will be followed by an exchange of views and discussions.

ARTICLE 2

Duration/Termination

The present agreement shall take effect as from 1st May 1988:- the various clauses contained therein are of a trial nature and will be re-examined by the signatories at the end of the two-year period.

Furthermore, should there be a substantial modification of the principal factors which have determined the conclusion of this agreement, the signatories agree to meet again without delay, at the request of one of the parties, in order to see what steps should be taken.

The present agreement will be declared null and void in the event of notice of termination being served in respect of the provisions contained in the agreement of 1st May 1988 concerning the setting up of the Central Works Council for the French companies in the BULL Group by one of the signatory parties to that agreement.

ARTICLE 3

Registration

The present agreement has been drawn up and signed as follows:-

in five signed copies for the Direction Départementale du Travail et de l'Emploi de Paris (Area Office of the Ministry of Labour and Employment) - 109 rue Montmartre, 75002 PARIS)

in one signed copy for the Secrétariat greffe du Conseil des Prud'hommes de Paris (Record Office of the Conciliation/Arbitration Board) - 84/86 Boulevard de Sébastopol, 75003 PARIS

in one additional copy to be kept by the Management of the BULL Group.

A copy of the agreement will be given to each of the signatory trade union organisations.

Paris, 22nd March 1988

For and on behalf of the Management :

C.F.E. - C.G.C.

C.F.D.T.

C.F.T.C.

C.G.T

C.G.T. - F. O.

(October 1985)

PROTOCOL AGREEMENT
====================================

THOMSON GRAND PUBLIC - EUROPEAN METALWORKERS' FEDERATION

LIAISON COMMITTEE

Taking into account the supranational character of the activities of the THOMSON GRAND PUBLIC Division, the signatories agree to set up a Liaison Committee, which will provide economic data on the industrial and trading situation with regard to THOMSON GRAND PUBLIC operations in Europe.

I - COMPOSITION

- The Managing Director of the firm THOMSON GRAND PUBLIC or his representative, together with the managers concerned.

- 15 representatives of trade unions organisations affiliated to the European Metalworkers' Federation (E.M.F.).

II - ALLOCATION OF SEATS

- 1 seat is reserved for a representative of the European Metalworkers' Federation.

- 14 seats are attributed to the representatives of trade union organisations affiliated to the E.M.F., or represented by the E.M.F., appointed from among the employees of this Division.

They are allocated as follows:-

- 6 seats for the French organisations
- 4   "   "   " German organisations
- 2   "   "   " Italian organisations
- 2   "   "   " Spanish organisations

III - PROCEDURE

The Committee will meet every six months on THOMSON GRAND PUBLIC or E.M.F. initiative, notice being given six weeks in advance.

The venue for the meeting will be chosed by THOMSON GRAND PUBLIC, which will meet all interpretation costs.

The travel and accommodation costs incurred by participants in these meetings will be met by the E.M.F.

All persons appointed who are employed in the THOMSON GRAND PUBLIC Division will be guaranteed payment of full wages during attendance of sessions of the European Committee.

Participants' names must be communicated to THOMSON GRAND PUBLIC at least two weeks before each meeting.

One of the two annual meetings must precede the annual session of the European Branch Commitee.

IV - COMPETENCE

The Liaison Committee shall be informed of the economic, industrial and trading activities of THOMSON GRAND PUBLIC.

It will be informed, prior to the implementation, of major structural, industrial and trading modifications and changes in the economic and legal organisation of THOMSON GRAND PUBLIC.

It will be informed of measures taken and planned for adapting the organisation and workforce to technological change as well as adapting employees' skills in the light of employment problems.

The members of the Liaison Committee may express opinions, in the light of the information supplied, on all the areas defined above.

V - The E.M.F. is to have access to the documents transmitted to the European Branch Committee.

It undertakes to respect the confidential or secret nature of these documents, as the case may be, vis-à-vis third parties.

VI - This protocol is concluded, on an experimental basis, for a period of two years as from 1st January 1986. The parties shall meet in the three months preceding its expiration in order to decide whether or not to renew these provisions.

            PARIS
            7th October 1985

EUROPEAN METALWORKERS' FEDERATION

represented by
Hubert THIERRON

THOMSON GRAND PUBLIC

represented by
Jean-Jacques PEUCH-LESTRADE

F.U.L.C. I.G. METALL C.F.D.T. C.G.T.-F.O. U.G.T.

(December 1987)

PROTOCOL AGREEMENT

THOMSON GRAND PUBLIC - EUROPEAN METALWORKERS' FEDERATION
LIAISON COMMITTEE

Taking into account the supranational character of the activities of the THOMSON GRAND PUBLIC Division, the signatories agree to set up a Liaison Committee, which will provide economic data on the industrial, commercial and research situation of THOMSON GRAND PUBLIC operations in Europe.

I - COMPOSITION

- The Managing Director of the firm THOMSON GRAND PUBLIC or his representative; together with the managers concerned.

- 13 representatives of trade unions organizations affiliated to the European Metalworkers' Federation (E.M.F.).

II - ALLOCATION OF SEATS

- 1 seat is reserved for a representative of the European Metalworkers' Federation.

- 12 seats are attributed to the representatives of trade union organizations affiliated to the E.M.F., or represented by the E.M.F., appointed from among employees of THOMSON GRAND PUBLIC or its subsidiaries or among full-time union Secretaries of the above-mentioned Organizations.

- They are allocated as follows :

    - 4 seats are reserved for the French Organizations ;
    - 3 seats   "   "   "   the German Organization ;
    - 2 seats   "   "   "   the British Organizations ;
    - 2 seats   "   "   "   the Italian Organization ;
    - 1 seat is   "   "   the Spanish Organization.

III - PROCEDURE

The Committe will meet once a year on either THOMSON GRAND PUBLIC or E.M.F. initiative. With the agreement of both parties, the Committe may meet on an ad hoc basis, even in a restricted form.
Notice must be given six weeks in advance.

The venue for the meeting will be chosen by THOMSON GRAND PUBLIC, which will meet all interpretation costs.

All persons appointed, who are employed by the THOMSON GRAND PUBLIC Division and its subsidiaries will be guaranteed payment of full wages during attendance of sessions of the European Committee and will be reimbursed ,by their employers, for the travelling and accommodation expenses incurred during attendance at these sessions.

Participants' names muts be communicated to THOMSON GRAND PUBLIC at least two weeks before each meeting.

The annual meeting must precede the annual session of the European Branch Committee.

IV - COMPETENCE

The Liaison Committee shall be informed of the economic, industrial, trading and research activities of THOMSON GRAND PUBLIC.

It will be informed, prior to the implementation, of major structural, industrial and trading modifications and changes in the economic and legal organization of THOMSON GRAND PUBLIC.

It will be informed of measures taken and planned for adapting the organization and workforce to technological change as well as adapting employees' skills in the light of employment problems.

The members of the Liaison Committee may express opinions, in the light of the information supplied, on all the areas defined above.

V - The E.M.F is to have access to the documents transmitted to the European Branch Committee.

It undertakes to respect the confidential or secret nature of these documents, as the case may be, vis-à-vis third parties.

VI - This protocol is concluded for an indertermined period to begin on the 1st of Januar 1988 and may be denounced by either party on 15 months notice.

Should there be important changes in the distribution of employees of THOMSON GRAND PUBLIC, this agreement may be revised on 9 months notice.

VII - The French text shall be the sole authoritative of this agreement.

             Paris,
             22th December 1987

EUROPEAN METALWORKERS'   THOMSON GRAND PUBLIC
FEDERATION
represented by   represented by
Hubert THIERRON   Jean-Jacques PEUCH-LESTRADE

FGMM-CFDT   CGT-FO   IG Metall   UGT-Metal
       Metallurgie

FILCEA/CGIL   UILCID/UIL   FLERICA/CISL

ASTMS   TASS   TGWU et ACTSS

AEU   EETPU   EETPU-EESA

(December 1989)

DRAFT AGREEMENT
THOMSON CONSUMER ELECTRONICS
EUROPEAN METALWORKERS' FEDERATION
LIAISON COMMITTEE

PURSUANT TO the agreement dated December 22 1987 between, on the one hand, THOMSON GRAND PUBLIC and on the other, the European Metalworkers' Federation and national Federations affiliated to the EMF, setting up a liaison committee,

WHEREAS THOMSON ELECTROMENAGER is no longer a part of THOMSON CONSUMER ELECTRONICS, which has superseded THOMSON GRAND PUBLIC for consumer electronics activities,

IT IS AGREED that the composition of the delegation of labor organizations adhering to the EMF shall be modified as follows:

- 1 seat remains reserved for a representative of the Eureopean Metalworkers' Federation

- 11 seats are allocated to representatives of organizations adhering to or represented by the EMF designated from among the employees of THOMSON CONSUMER ELECTRONICS or its European subsidiaries or from among full-time union secretaries of the above-mentioned organizations.

They are allocated as follows :

- 3 seats for the French organizations
- 3 seats for the German organization
- 2 seats for the British organizations
- 2 seats for the Italian organization
  1 seat for the Spanish organization.

Otherwise, the agreement dated December 22 1987 remains unchanged.

The French text shall constitute the only authoritative version of this agreement.

Paris, December 18 1989

EUROPEAN METALWORKERS' FEDERATION
Represented by
Hubert THIERRON

THOMSON CONSUMER ELECTRONICS
Represented by
Pierre ALLAIN

FULC

FGMM-CFDT

FO Métallurgie

EETPU

AEU

IG Metall

UGT-Metal

(October 1985)

PROTOCOL AGREEMENT

EUROPEAN BRANCH COMMITTEE

Considering the European character of the activities of the THOMSON GRAND PUBLIC Division, the signatories agree to set up a European Branch Committee, which is a new institution that must not lead to a diminution of the role of the French Branch Committee resulting from the agreement of 28th February 1984 signed with the representative French trade union organisations at THOMSON GRAND PUBLIC Division level.

This body must provide information for representatives of personnel employed in the THOMSON GRAND PUBLIC Division, at European level, on its economic, industrial and trading situation.

I - COMPOSITION

- The Managing Director of the firm THOMSON GRAND PUBLIC or his representative, together with the managers concerned.
- 26 employee representatives appointed by the representative trade union organisations in France, Italy and Spain, at the Division level, from among the elected members of the Works Committees or Councils of subsidiaries of THOMSON GRAND PUBLIC and, in the case of the Federal Republic of Germany, by the Central Works Councils or, failing this, by the Works Councils.

II - ALLOCATION OF SEATS

In order to counter any disparities that may result from strict application of the rule of proportional representation in relation to the number of employees, each country will be represented, a priori, by 2 employee representatives.

Allocation of the other seats will be in proportion to the number of employees in the Division in the four European countries concerned, i.e. currently France, Germany, Italy and Spain.

On the basis of the total workforce as at 30th June 1985, employees of subsidiaries are to be represented as follows:-

- French subsidiaries are represented by 13 members
- German   "   "   "   by 8   "
- Italian   "   "   "   by 3   "
- Spanish   "   "   "   by 2   "

The employee representatives of each country will be appointed, as laid down in paragraph I, in accordance with the number of elected council members, as per the tables annexed to this protocol.

III - PROCEDURE

The Branch Committee will meet once per year and will be convened by the management of THOMSON GRAND PUBLIC.

An ad hoc Committee may be constituted in respect of each problem liable to modify the industrial and trading position of the Division at European level. At its first meeting, the European Branch Committee will determine all details regarding the setting-up and operation of the ad hoc Committees.

The meeting costs (room and interpretation, as well as the accommodation and travel expenses incurred in respect of attendance of this meeting) will be met by THOMSON GRAND PUBLIC.

Employee representatives will be guaranteed payment of full wages for the duration of the meeting.

The names of the members of the European Branch Committee will be communicated to THOMSON GRAND PUBLIC by the appropriate bodies as per paragraph I before 31st December 1985.

The members of the European Branch Committee shall hold office for a period of two years.

During the two-year period of office, no other appointment may be made except in the following cases:-

- Departure from the company or Division
- Change in trade union affiliation
- Loss of seat on a Works Committee or (Central) Works Council
- For the Federal Republic of Germany:- Removal from appointed post by the Central Works Council or, failing this, the Works Council following the said Council's declared loss of confidence.

IV - COMPETENCE

The European Branch Committee will be informed of the Division's economic, industrial and trading activities in Europe and of the measures taken and planned for adapting personnel of subsidiaries in the countries concerned to technological change and adapting their skills in the light of employment problems.

The European Branch Committee will be informed, prior to implementation, of all major structural and industrial changes provided the decision is taken at Division level.

The European Branch Committee will be informed of economic and legal organisational changes in the Division (acquisition or transfer of subsidiaries).

V - The present protocol is concluded, on an experimental basis, for a period of two years as from 1st January 1986. The parties will meet in the three months preceding its expiration in order to decide whether or not to renew these provisions.

PARIS
7th October 1985

French trade union organisations

For and on behalf of the firm
THOMSON GRAND PUBLIC

C.F.D.T.
C.G.C.
C.G.T.
C.G.T.-F.O.

Jean-Jacques PEUCH-LESTRADE

German Works Council or Central Works Council members

GBR NEWEK
GBR DEWEK
GBR SADA
GBR TELEFUNKEN
GBR DAGFU
GBR NORDMENDE

Italian trade union organisations

F.U.L.C.

Spanish trade union organisations

U.G.T.
C.G.O.O.

European Metalworkers' Federation

WORKS COUNCIL ELECTION RESULTS

COUNTRY	NAME OF UNION	NO. ELECTED	NO. OF SEATS
FRANCE		161	13
	C.G.T.	63	6
	C.F.D.T.	56	5
	F.O.	18	1
	C.F.T.C.	4	-
	C.G.C.	20	1
ITALY		21	3
	C.G.I.L.	15	)
	C.I.S.L.	2	) 3
	U.I.L.	4	)
SPAIN		17	2
	C.G.O.O.	8	1
	U.G.T.	5	1
	N.A.	4	-
GERMANY		54	8
	I.G. METALL	33	7
	D.A.G.	4	1
	O. G.	17	-

(April 1988)

PROTOCOL AGREEMENT

EUROPEAN BRANCH COMMISSION

In view of the European nature of the activities of THOMSON GRAND PUBLIC, the undersigned agree on the existence of a European Branch Commission. This body will in no way diminish the role of the French Branch Commission created on the basis of an agreement signed by THOMSON GRAND PUBLIC with the relevant French trade unions on February 28, 1984 at the activities of THOMSON GRAND PUBLIC level.

This body shall keep the staff delegates of THOMSON GRAND PUBLIC informed, at the European level, of the financial, industrial, commercial and research position.

I - MEMBERS

- The President and Chief Executive Officer of THOMSON GRAND PUBLIC or his representatives, assisted by the relevant Directors.

- 26 staff delegates appointed by the representative trade unions :

    . in France, Italy, Spain and the United Kingdom at the THOMSON GRAND PUBLIC activities level from among the selected members of the Office or Works Councils or Committees (Comités ou Conseils d'Entreprise) of the subsidiaries ;

    . in the Federal Republic of Germany : by the Central Office or Works Councils (Conseils Centraux d'Entreprise) or by the Office or Works Councils (Conseils d'Entreprise) of the five different sectors of activity and industry.

II - ALLOCATION OF SEATS

In order to avoid any imbalance which might result from strictly proportional representation, each country will be automatically represented by 2 staff delegates.

Allocation of the remaining seats will be proportional to the work force in the five countries : France, Germany, Italy, Spain and United Kingdom.

According to figures at October 30, 1987, the subsidiairies will be represented by :

- France   : 13 members
- Germany   :   5   "
- Italy   :   3   "
- United Kingdom :   3   "
- Spain   :   2   "

Staff delegates from each country will be appointed, as indicated in paragraph 1, according to the number of elected members of the Office or Works Councils or Committees (Comité ou Conseils d'Entreprise), as listed in the tables appended to this Protocol Agreement.

III - WORKING PROCEDURE

The Branch Commission will be convened by the Executive of THOMSON GRAND PUBLIC once a year.

Ad hoc committees may be organised to consider any problem which may modify the industrial and commercial position at european level. The European Branch Commission will decide then on the procedures for setting up and running the ad hoc committees.

Expenses (meeting room, interpreting, travel and accomodation expenses) incurred by the meeting will be paid by THOMSON GRAND PUBLIC.

Salaries of staff delegates will continue to be paid throughout the period of the meeting.

The names of the members of the European Branch Commission are to be submitted to THOMSON GRAND PUBLIC by the relevant parties, as indicated in paragraph 1, for the first time before March 31, 1988.

Staff delegates' term of office to the European Branch Commission will be 2 years. At the expiry of this period, the signatories will decide the allocation of seats according to the allocation of the workforce and the number of elected members in the different countries.

During any given 2-year term of office, no new appointment may be made except in the following cases :

- departure from the Company or from the THOMSON GRAND PUBLIC activities

- change of trade union affiliation

- defeat in an Office or Works Councils or Committees (Comités ou Conseils d'Entreprise) election

- in the case of the Federal Republic of Germany, revocation of an appointment by the Central Office or Works Councils (Conseils Centraux d'Entreprise) or by the Office or Works Councils (Conseils d'Entreprise), following a vote of non-confidence by the aforementioned council.

IV - AREA OF JURIDICTION

The European Branch Commission will be informed of the financial, industrial, commercial and research activity of THOMSON GRAND PUBLIC in Europe. It will be notified of measures taken or considered for adapting the personnel of subsidiairies of the countries involved to technological developments, and of personnel qualifications as regards employment problems.

The European Branch Commission will be informed, before their implementation, of any significant structural or industrial modifications, if the decision is to be made at the level of THOMSON GRAND PUBLIC.

The European Branch Commission will be informed of any modifications to the economic or legal organisation of The THOMSON GRAND PUBLIC activities (acquisition or sale of subsidiairies).

V - This protocol is concluded for an indertermined period to begin on the 1st of Januar 1988.

Should there be important changes in the distribution of employees of THOMSON GRAND PUBLIC, this agreement may be revised on 9 months notice.

VI - The French text shall be the sole authoritative of this agreement.

Paris,

For THOMSON GRAND PUBLIC,
Jean-Jacques PEUCH-LESTRADE

The French trade Unions :

C.F.D.T.

C.F.T.C.

C.G.C.

C.G.T.

C.G.T.-F.O.

The German Members :

The Italian trade unions :

F.U.L.C.

The Spanish trade unions :

U.G.T.

C.G.O.O.

The British unions :

The European Metalworkers' Federation :

DRAFT AGREEMENT
EUROPEAN COMMISSION
OF
THOMSON CONSUMER ELECTRONICS

PURSUANT to the draft agreement dated October 7 1985,

PURSUANT to the draft agreement dated April 6 1988,

WHEREAS home appliance activities have been separated from consumer electronics,

WHEREAS from March 29 1989 THOMSON ELECTROMENAGER is attached directly to THOMSON S.A.,

WHEREAS from January 1 1989 THOMSON CONSUMER ELECTRONICS has superseded THOMSON GRAND PUBLIC for consumer electronics activities,

IT IS AGREED that the composition of the European Commission of THOMSON CONSUMER ELECTRONICS shall be modified.

This modification shall affect neither the role nor the operation of said institution.

I/ COMPOSITION

The European Commission of THOMSON CONSUMER ELECTRONICS is composed :

- on the one hand, of the Chairman and Chief Executive Officer of THOMSON CONSUMER ELECTRONICS or his representative, assisted by the directors concerned,

- on the other hand, of 20 representatives of the staff of THOMSON CONSUMER ELECTRONICS or its European subsidiaries designated by representative labor organizations in France, Italy, Spain and the United

Kingdom from among the elected members of works councils or committees, and, in the case of the Federal Republic of Germany, by central works councils or, failing this, by the works councils of the various industrial and other activities.

II/ ALLOCATION OF SEATS

In order to avoid any discrepancies arising from strict application of a rule of proportional representation according to headcount, each country shall be represented <u>a priori</u> by two staff representatives.

Remainning seats shall be allocated in proportion to headcount in the five European countries currently concerned, namely France, Germany, Italy, Spain and the United Kingdom.

In accordance with headcount at February 2 1989, seats are allocated as follows :

- France   : 6 members
- Germany : 6 members
- UK   : 3 members
- Italy   : 3 members
- Spain   : 2 members

Staff representatives for each country shall be designated as laid out in paragraph I according to the number of elected representatives (see tables in appendix).

III/ PROCEDURE

The European Commission of THOMSON CONSUMER ELECTRONICS shall meet once per year at the initiative of the Management.

The Commission may meet on an ad hoc basis for any problem likely to modify the industrial or commercial situation at

European level. Details for setting up an ad hoc Commission and procedures shall be determined by the European Commission.

Meeting expenses (room and interpreting facilities, travel and living expenses) shall be paid by THOMSON CONSUMER ELECTRONICS.

Staff representatives shall be guaranteed full wages during the meeting.

Names of members of the European Commission shall be communicated to THOMSON CONSUMER ELECTRONICS by the authorities laid down in paragraph I, for the first time, before December 31 1989.

The mandate period for members of the European Commission is two years. At the end of this period, the signatory parties shall decide on the allocation of seats according to headcount and the number of elected representatives in each country.

New designations may not be made during the two-year mandate, with the following exceptions :

- departure from THOMSON CONSUMER ELECTRONICS or one of its European subsidiaries
- loss of mandate at (central) works council or committee level
- for the Federal Republic of Germany, withdrawal of designation by the Central Council or, where necessary, by the Works Council, following a loss of confidence declared by the Council.

IV/ COMPETENCE

The European Commission of THOMSON CONSUMER ELECTRONICS shall be informed of the economical, industrial, commercial and research activities of THOMSON CONSUMER ELECTRONICS in Europe, and of measures taken or envisaged, so as to adapt the staff of THOMSON CONSUMER ELECTRONICS and its European subsidiaries to developments in technology and their qualifications in face of employment problems.

The European Commission shall be informed in advance of major structural or industrial changes when decisions are taken at THOMSON CONSUMER ELECTRONICS level.

The European Commission shall be informed of any changes in the organization of the activities of THOMSON CONSUMER ELECTRONICS (purchase or sale of subsidiaries).

V/ The French text shall constitute the sole authoritative version of this agreement.

Paris, January 19 1990

For THOMSON CONSUMER ELECTRONICS
Pierre ALLAIN

For the LABOR ORGANIZATIONS

MSS

EETPU

FOR EUROPEAN METALWORKERS'FEDERATION

EUROPEAN COMMISSION

HEADCOUNT / NUMBER OF SEATS PER COUNTRY

COUNTRY	HEADCOUNT	SEATS
FEDERAL REPUBLIC OF GERMANY	4.850	6
FRANCE	4.170	6
UNITED-KINGDOM	2.800	3
ITALY	2.300	3
SPAIN	1.200	2
TOTAL		20

(July 1991)

SOCIETE NATIONALE ELF AQUITAINE

AGREEMENT REGARDING THE ESTABLISHMENT AND THE RUNNING

OF A EUROPEAN INFORMATION AND CONCERTATION BODY

In the general framework of the construction of Europe, the Community Charter on Fundamental Social Rights provides that "information, consultation and participation for workers must be developed along appropriate lines, taking account of the practices in force in the various Member States".

To this effect and even before these principles become enshrined in Community legislation, the management of the Elf Aquitaine Group, following negociations with union organizations, undertakes to establish an appropriate body, provisionally named the European Information and concertation Body.

In signing this agreement, the parties to it express their common determination to promote, at European level, a constructive social dialogue, based, as defined in Community documents, on Information and consultation of workers in the areas which concern Elf Aquitaine and its employees.

Any other european or national union organization having employee representative status in any of the Group's European companies and falling within the scope of application of this agreement, will be able to become a party to it. In any case, the agreement will be applicable to all these companies.

Article 1 - PURPOSE AND OBJECT

The European Information and concertation Body is a structure for discussion and dialogue. It will deal with and debate - at European level - economic, financial and social issues, and prospects whose consequences for the activities of the companies concerned, render their study necessary on account of their general character and the context in which they arise.

The Body should permit debate and expression at the European level of the views of the different participants, notably with regard to the following matters :

- ECONOMIC

Organization and operations, Group strategic plans, general trends in technical matters, research and development policy, etc...

- FINANCIAL

Annual budgets and balance sheets, Group consolidated financial statements, etc...

- HUMAN RESOURCES

Employment policy (volume, structure, forecasts, etc...)

The role of the Body will be to supplement the work of similar national bodies. Under no circumstances may it substitute for them or impair the rights of employees and their representatives in each country.

Article 2 - SCOPE OF APPLICATION

Personnel concerned are those working in any unit located in the Member-States of the European Economic Community and the European Free Trade Area, under the payroll of a company having its headquarters in any such country and whose share capital is held, directly or indirectly, in excess of 50 % by Société Nationale Elf Aquitaine.

Article 3 - MEMBERSHIP

The European Information and concertation Body will comprise :

a) on the one hand, the Chairman and Chief Executive Officer of Société Nationale Elf Aquitaine, assisted inter alia by the following executives :

- the Senior Vice President, Human Resources
- The Senior Vice President, Finance
- The Senior Vice President, Planning and Strategy
- The Chief Operating Officer of each Group Division.

b) and on the other hand

- forty five representatives of the personnel of European subsidiaries excluding France

- thirty representatives of the personnel of french subsidiaries, and the five French Group Union Coordinators.

The appendix to this agreement sets forth the principles and procedures governing the nomination of representatives of european subsidiaries personnel as well as the rules for apportionment of such nominations. Every effort will be made to ensure that the different professional categories of personnel and the different employees representations trends, are properly represented.

Article 4 : REPRESENTATIVES OF NON EEC EUROPEAN SUBSIDIARIES

Representatives of the personnel of non EEC European subsidiaries will attend meetings of the information and concertation Body as full members, except with regard to those matters dealing specifically with the application of Community legislation, in which case they shall attend as observers.

Article 5 - MEETINGS

The European Information and concertation Body will meet once a year, upon notice given by its Chairman. If circumstances require, an other extraordinary meeting may be called in the same year.

Organizational and procedural rules and principles governing these meetings are defined in the appendix.

The management of a Group division may eventually convene a yearly meeting with regard to its own specific activities, in accordance with such rules which it will have to define within this Group division.

Article 6 - TRANSITIONAL ARRANGEMENTS

One month at the latest prior to the first meeting, the Human Resources Management will advise the signatories and the Group Union Coordinators of the conditions under which the appointment of representatives has been made and followed up by each Group division.

The European Information and concertation Body will function initially on a transitional basis for a period of two years following the first meeting.

As the end of the first meeting, the Management and representatives of the signatories will review the running of the Body. At the end of the transitional period, conditions for renewal and running of the Body will be reviewed, taking into consideration in particular the development and the level of the Group activities in Europe.

In any case, such procedural rules and principles which will have been agreed, will be reviewed in the light of changes in Community legislation.

Article 7 - PUBLICATION

Pending the enactment of a European Community legislation on the legal status of collective agreements, the applicable laws to this agreement will be these of the State where the headquarters of Société Nationale Elf Aquitaine are located.

These heads of agreement will be registered with the clark of the "Tribunal des Prud'hommes" in Nanterre, and with the "Direction Départementale du Travail" (Department of Labor) of the region "Hauts de Seine".

A copy of the same will be sent to the Commission of the European Communities.

Courbevoie, 19th july 1991

Signatories thereafter

At the European level :

At the national level :

The union organizations under-mentionned, affiliated to the European Trade Union Confederation (ETUC) through their national confederations, and represented, for their industrial sectors, by the EFCGU :

For France :

-
-
-
-
-
-

-
-
-
-
-

For........................

-

The union organizations under-mentionned, affiliated to the "Confédération Européenne des Cadres" (CEC) through their national confederations, and represented, for their industrial sectors, by the FICCIA :

-
-
-
-

-
-
-
-
-

The Chairman and Chief Executive Officer
of the Société Nationale Elf Aquitaine

Loïk LE FLOCH-PRIGENT

(Please, see the Agreement written in french)

APPENDIX TO THE AGREEMENT OF 19th July 1991

REGARDING THE ESTABLISHMENT AND THE RUNNING OF A EUROPEAN

INFORMATION AND CONCERTATION BODY

This appendix lays down the general principles pertaining to the establishment and running of the European Information and concertation Body regardind the following items:

I - <u>Representatives of personnel of European subsidiaries excluding France</u>

1.1 - <u>Apportionment</u>

The nominations of representatives of employees of European subsidiaries - excluding France - will be apportioned in accordance with the table attached hereto and drawn up according to the following criteria :

* The different Group divisions should be equally represented with 15 representatives per division

* For any given division, each country employing at least 50 people of national status will be represented by one or more delegates, depending on the size of the workforce and the scale of the different activities.

1.2 - <u>Appointment</u>

Representatives of employees of European subsidiaries - excluding France - will be appointed for all the subsidiaries of a given Group division in each country, according to the paragraphs hereafter 1.2.1, 1.2.2 and 1.2.3. The Management of each Group Division is responsible for the right organization of the appointment, in accordance with the agreement.

Inside a given country and division, the managers of the subsidiaries may be represented by a "coordinator".

Personnel representatives who are members of the Body must be employed by a European subsidiary of the Group, falling within the scope of application defined in Article 2 of the agreement, and must, in principle, be elected representatives of the personnel or union officials.

The personnel representative's mandate is incompatible with the function of Chief Executive Officer, or any related function in regard to the personnel.

Deputy delegates will be appointed according to the same procedures in order to substitute for the full members, should the latter be unable to attend the meetings.

Owing to the diversity of situations at national levels, appointments should be made in accordance with the following general principles :

1.2.1) Existing employees representation in the subsidiaries

For any given Group division, the managers of the subsidiaries or the coordinator will turn to personnel representatives and, if in keeping with local procedures, to the delegates of union organizations represented in the company in order to notify them of the conditions in which the European Information and concertation Body is to be established (nature and purpose of the Body, procedural arrangements, etc...) and invite them to communicate the name of the applicant (or applicants) for the post (or posts) to be filled.

These representatives will be given the necessary means to contact their union organization and to attend a meeting in their country and within their division in order to allow candidates to come forward.

Names of candidates will be communicated to the managers of subsidiaries or to the coordinator who will testify :

- either that the number of candidates corresponds to the number of posts to be filled, in which case all the candidates will be deemed to be appointed.

- or that the number of candidates is greater than provided for. In which case, if no agreement can be reached, the union organizations signatories to the agreement will be notified accordingly, and thereafter the representatives will be elected either by a vote of all personnel representatives, or by a vote of the employees themselves.

1.2.2) No employees representation existing in all subsidiaries concerned

If no personnel representation exists, the union organizations signatories to the agreement will be notified accordingly, and thereafter candidates from all the subsidiaries in the country and the Group division concerned will be invited to come forward and all the employees will proceed to a vote.

1.2.3) Possible adjustments to appointment procedures

If the above general appointment procedures are incompatible with specific national legislation, procedures or other local considerations, the union organizations signatories will be notified accordingly, and thereafter adjustments may be agreed at the level of the subsidiaries concerned.

II - Appointment of personnel representatives in the French subsidiaries

The thirty representatives of the employees of French subsidiaries must be under the payroll of a French subsidiary of the Group, falling within the scope of application as defined in Article 2 of the agreement. They will be designated by the union officials represented at national and Group levels, on the basis of ten per Group division.

They must, in principle, be either an elected representative of the personnel or a union official.

These thirty posts will be broken down as follows :

- one for each union organization and for each Group division, amounting to a total of fifteen

- fifteen further posts determined in proportion to the results of the latest elections of the representatives of employees to the Board of Directors of Société Nationale Elf Aquitaine.

Similarly, these union organizations will appoint an equivalent number of deputy representatives in order to substitute for the full members of the Body, should the latter fail to attend the meetings.

III - Meetings

Each plenary meeting will be preceded the previous day by preparatory meetings. The required facilities will be made available (meeting rooms and necessary simultaneous translation devices). Deputy representatives will attend the said meetings only in-so-far as the full members fail to attend.

The Body will appoint a secretary from among its members. This person will be responsible for drafting the minutes of the meetings, and will be given the means and time required. He will be assisted in this by the administrative secretary of the "Comité de Groupe", who will attend the meetings of the Body.

The agenda will be set by the Chairman and the secretary. It will be communicated, together with the appropriate background documents, to each of the members twenty days at the latest prior to the meeting, except in exceptional circumstances.

Personnel representatives at the Body will be entitled to be assisted by the Group Committee's certified public accountant at both preparatory and plenary meetings.

They will be entitled also to be assisted, for preparatory meetings, by an expert who will be designated preferably from among the employees of Group companies, subject however to the nature of the questions discussed, and to the prior approval of the management. In this case, corresponding travel and accomodation costs will be borne by the Company.

Simultaneous translation will be made available in all the European languages required to allow the participants to follow the proceedings properly. Preparatory documents and minutes will be drafted in French and English.

Personnel representatives in the Body will be given the necessary means to perform their tasks adequately (including internal documents and sufficient time to study these documents). These means will be determined by the Management of the subsidiary to which each representative belongs, in concertation with Management of the Group division and whoever is concerned.

Travel and accomodation costs and expenses for time spent in connection with the Body will be borne by the company to which the representative belongs according to the procedures existing in this company.

EUROPEAN INFORMATION AND CONCERTATION BODY

Representatives of Employees

	Hydrocarbons Division	Chemicals Division	Heath, Beauty products and bio-activities Division
BELGIUM	2	1	2
DENMARK	-	-	-
GERMANY	2	4	2
GREECE	-	-	1
IRELAND	-	-	-
ITALY	2	3	3
LUXEMBOURG	-	-	-
NETHERLANDS	2	2	1
PORTUGAL	-	-	1
SPAIN	1	2	2
UNITED KINGDOM	3	2	2
AUSTRIA	-	-	-
NORWAY	2	-	-
SWITZERLAND	1	1	1
TOTAL	15	15	15
FRANCE	10	10	10

EUROPEAN INFORMATION AND CONCERTATION BODY

Representatives of employees of French subsidiaries

	Hydrocarbons Division	Chemicals Division	Health, Beauty Products, and Bio-Activities Division
CFDT	3	2	2
CFE-CGC	2	2	2
CFTC	1	?	1
CGT	2	3	3
CGT-FO	2	1	2
TOTAL	10	10	10

BSN GROUPE

RELATIONS HUMAINES
LE DIRECTEUR GENERAL

Monsieur Dan GALLIN
Secrétaire Général de
l'U.I.T.A.
8, rampe du Pont-rouge
CH-1213 PETIT-LANCY (GENEVE)

- Suisse -

Paris, le 17 juin 1986

Monsieur le Secrétaire Général,

A votre invitation, Monsieur RIBOUD est venu le 21 avril dernier à Genève présenter le Groupe BSN aux responsables des organisations affiliées à l'U.I.T.A.. A l'issue de cette rencontre, nous sommes convenus de la poursuite de ces relations et nous nous sommes réunis le 9 juin à Paris pour en examiner les modalités.

Suite à ces conversations, nous vous proposons de procéder de la façon suivante :

- Organiser, dans une première étape, pendant les deux années prochaines, une rencontre annuelle des syndicats européens affiliés à l'U.I.T.A. de la Direction Générale du Groupe BSN.

- Cette rencontre, d'une journée, réunira un représentant par syndicat affilié à l'U.I.T.A. dans les pays d'Europe où BSN est implanté (Italie, Espagne, Belgique, Allemagne, Pays-Bas, Autriche, France), ainsi que des représentants du S.E.T.A. et de l'U.I.T.A., soit une quinzaine de personnes.

- Pourront y participer également une quinzaine de syndicalistes salariés des sociétés du Groupe BSN, dont la liste aura été communiquée préalablement à la Direction Générale de BSN. Les journées d'absence ces participants pour ces réunions seront considérées comme journées travail. Leurs temps de déplacements, leurs frais de déplacements et d'hébergement seront traités par leurs sociétés d'origine selon les règles en vigueur dans celles-ci.

- Cette rencontre sera préparée par un groupe restreint comprenant des représentants du S.E.T.A. et de l'U.I.T.A. ainsi que de la Direction Générale de BSN.

- BSN accepte de prendre sa part des frais de location de salle et de traduction des débats.

- Pour mettre en oeuvre ces dispositions, décider des sujets à traiter pendant ces deux années, et préparer la première rencontre annuelle, une réunion est prévue dans la dernière semaine d'octobre 1986, à Bruxelles ou à Luxembourg, avec les représentants des syndicats européens affiliés à l'U.I.T.A..

Ces rencontres doivent nous permettre de nous informer réciproquement et ainsi de faire progresser les relations sociales dans les sociétés européennes du Groupe BSN.

Dans cette attente,

Je vous prie d'agréer, Monsieur le Secrétaire Général, l'expression de mes salutations distinguées.

Antoine MARTIN
Directeur Général
des Relations Humaines

c.c. M. Otto STAADT

Translation of letter to M. Dan Gallin, General Secretary of IUF, from M. Antoine Martin, Head of Human Relations at BSN, dated 17 June 1986

Dear Sir

At your invitation, M. Riboud travelled to Geneva on 21 April last to introduce the BSN group to senior officers of those organisations affiliated to the IUF. Following this meeting, we agreed to continue the links forged and met in Paris on 9 June to discuss practicalities.

Further to that meeting, we now have pleasure in suggesting the following plan for progress.

As a first stage, we suggest that over the next two years, the European trade unions affiliated to the IUF should meet the general management of the BSN group on an annual basis. This would be an all-day meeting involving one representative from each of the unions affiliated to the IUF in those European countries where BSN operates (ie Italy, Spain, Belgium, Germany, the Netherlands, Austria and France) plus representatives of the ECF and IUF themselves - a total of some 15 people.

The meeting would also be open to 15 or so white-collar trade unionists from BSN group companies provided that a list of names was submitted in advance to BSN's general management. The time employees spend attending these meetings would be deemed to be working time, and the costs arising from payment during absence and travel and accommodation costs would be met by their respective companies in line with normal custom and practice.

A small steering group, comprising ECF, IUF and BSN general management representatives, would be convened to make all the necessary arrangements for the meetings. BSN commits itself to meeting the room-hire and interpreting costs.

In order that these arrangements can be made in good time, it is envisaged that the subjects to be covered over the two year period be decided in the final week of October 1986 and arrangements made for the first meeting at the same time. This would be done in Brussels or Luxembourg, together with representatives of the European trade unions affiliated to the IUF.

These meetings should enable us to keep each other informed and to further industrial relations within the BSN group's European companies. In anticipation, I remain

yours faithfully

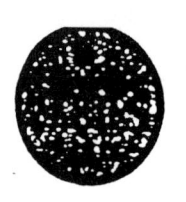

Monsieur Antoine MARTIN
Directeur Général des
Relations Humaines
Groupe BSN
7, rue de Téhéran
F - 75381 Paris Cedex 08

dg/pdm/51.533

Genève, le 24 juin 1986

Monsieur le Directeur Général,

Nous accusons réception de votre courrier du 17 juin qui concerne la forme de nos relations futures.

La réunion qui s'est tenue le 9 juin 1986 à Paris a permis de dégager les orientations générales que vous avez repris dans votre courrier, c'est-à-dire

- organisation d'une rencontre annuelle des syndicats affiliés à l'UITA et de la Direction générale du groupe BSN. Il s'agit pour l'essentiel de syndicats des pays européens, mais il est convenu que des responsables syndicaux d'autres pays peuvent assister à ce type de rencontre à titre d'observateurs

- composition de la délégation syndicale : environ 15 secrétaires syndicaux permanents et 15 syndicalistes salariés des sociétés du groupe BSN. Ces derniers verront leurs frais de déplacements et d'hébergement pris en charge par leurs sociétés d'origine selon les règles en vigueur dans celles-ci. Leurs journées d'absence seront considérées comme journées de travail. Assisteront également à cette réunion des représentants du secrétariat du SETA/UITA et de l'UITA.

- préparation de cette réunion plénière par un groupe de travail restreint comprenant des représentants du SETA/UITA, de l'UITA ainsi que de la direction générale. La première réunion de ce type, ouverte à l'ensemble des secrétaires nationaux européens, aura lieu le 29 octobre 1986 à Bruxelles.

Votre courrier du 17 juin 1986, ainsi que la présente réponse, définissent, à l'exception de tout autre document, le cadre formel de nos futures relations.

Veuillez agréer, Monsieur le Directeur Général, l'expression de ma considération distinguée.

Dan Gallin
Secrétaire Général

Translation of letter to M. Antoine Martin, Head of Human Relations at BSN, from M. Dan Gallin, General Secretary of the IUF, dated 24 June 1986

Dear Sir

We acknowledge receipt of your letter of 17 June concerning the format of our future relationship.

The meeting held in Paris on 9 June 1986 enabled us to lay down the broad outline set out in your letter, viz.:

- an annual meeting of the unions affiliated to the IUF with the general management of the BSN group. These will normally be trade unions from European countries, but it was agreed that trade union officers from other countries may attend such meetings as observers;

- the trade union delegation will comprise about 15 trade union officers and 15 white-collar trade union representatives from BSN group companies. The latter's travel and accommodation costs will be met by their respective companies, according to local custom and practice, and the time they spend away from their jobs for this purpose will be considered as working time. Representatives of the ECF/IUF secretariat and of the IUF will also attend;

- the plenary meeting will be organised by a small steering committee comprising ECF/IUF representatives, IUF representatives and representatives of the general management. The first such meeting, which will be open to all national secretaries in the European countries, will take place in Brussels on 29 October 1986.

Your letter of 17 June 1986, and this response, set out the formal framework for our future relationship unless otherwise explicitly laid down.

Yours faithfully

SYNDICAT C.G.T.
BSN
USINE de et à
88 - GIRONCOURT

COMMUNIQUE

C.N.T.
SECCIÓ SINDICAL
COMITE DE FABRICA
VIDRIERIA VILELLA, S.A.

Le syndicat CGT de Gironcourt et le syndicat CNT de Vidreria Vilella ESPAGNE se sont rencontrés le 10 OCTOBRE 1988 à Gironcourt, cette visite fait suite à l'absorption par BSN, à hauteur de 100 % du capital de la société Vidreria Vilella, ils situent la nécessité de voir les possibilités communes d'harmonisation d'accords pour les salariés appartenant au groupe BSN, ainsi que des relations nécessaires à avoir au niveau du verre d'emballage de BSN dans le cadre d'institutions légales et reconnues de représentativité des salariés au niveau de la société.

Les deux délégations présentes, ont fait un tour d'horizon des problèmes rencontrés au niveau de leur établissement respectif ainsi qu'au niveau de la filiale verre d'emballage de BSN dont Vidreria Vilella vient d'être intégré depuis Mai 1988.

Elles soulignent la nécessité de voir une structure de groupe leur permettant d'avoir des contacts dans un premier temps biannuel leur assurant la connaissance des données économiques et stratégiques de BSN emballage au niveau de l'Europe par l'intermédiaire d'une commission interentreprises verrière au niveau du groupe BSN.

Les deux délégations oeuvreront dans ce sens au niveau de leur direction respective afin de défendre en commun l'intérêt des salariés du verre travaillant dans la branche du verre d'emballage de BSN.

Elles reconnaissent l'intérêt de poursuivre de telles rencontres permettant de mieux situer les problèmes que rencontrent les salariés des différents établissements tant en Espagne qu'en France.

LE SYNDICAT CGT
GIRONCOURT

LE SYNDICAT CNT
VIDRERIA VILELLA

Translation of statement from the CGT union branch, Gironcourt, and the CNT union branch, Vidreria Vilella

The Gironcourt CGT union and the Vidreria Vilella (Spain) CNT union met on 10 October 1988 at Gironcourt following the takeover by BSN of 100% of the capital of Vidreria Vilella. The two unions held the meeting against the background of the need to explore joint opportunities to harmonise agreements for BSN group employees and also to explore the necessary links within the BSN glass packaging sector in terms of the statutory and negotiated employee representative bodies within the company.

The two delegations summarised the issues which had arisen at the level of each of the two plants and at the level of the BSN glass packaging subsidiary into which Vidreria Vilella had been incorporated in May 1988.

The delegations stress the need for a group structure which would enable them to meet initially on a biannual basis with access to economic and strategic information about BSN packaging in Europe through an inter-company committee for the glass sector within the BSN group.

To this end, the two delegations will work with their respective managements to jointly defend the position of glass workers with the BSN glass packaging sector.

They acknowledge the usefulness of continuing such meetings which enable them to have a better understanding of the issues facing the employees of the various plants in both Spain and France.

(Signed on behalf of both unions)

BSN GROUPE

BRANCHE EMBALLAGE
LE DIRECTEUR GENERAL

Monsieur les DRHS

A l'attention de

Paris, le 24 avril 1990

MTC/VA/

Monsieur,

Comme convenu lors de notre réunion du 3 avril 1990, je vous confirme que la Direction Générale de la Branche Emballage de BSN a décidé, suite à une demande de la CGT française et de la CNT (CGT) espagnole, et après avoir consulté le 3 avril 1990 les représentants des différents syndicats des sociétés verrières de BSN en Espagne, Hollande et France, de mettre en place une <u>commission d'information verrière européenne</u>.

Cette commission permettra aux participants de recevoir et d'échanger des informations sur la situation des sociétés verrières de la Branche, tant en matière économique (résultats, marchés, projets industriels, innovations technologiques) que sociale (conditions de travail, sécurité, formation). Elle n'est en aucune façon une instance de négociation. Elle ne doit pas empiéter sur les instances représentatives qui existent dans les sociétés.

Dans un premier temps cette expérience se déroulera selon les modalités suivantes :

- avec les représentants de la Direction Générale de la Branche Emballage, participeront à cette commission les 12 personnes qui ont été désignées par leurs syndicats pour la réunion du 3 avril 1990. Ces personnes pourront, si besoin est, se faire remplacer par un autre membre du même syndicat, salarié d'une des sociétés verrières du Groupe BSN, à condition d'en prévenir préalablement le DRHS de leur société,

- la première réunion de la commission se tiendra à Séville le 10 octobre 1990. Le 9 octobre après-midi, les 12 syndicalistes participant à la commission pourront tenir entre eux une réunion préparatoire. Des interprètes seront mis à leur disposition,

- les journées d'absence pour réunion seront considérées comme journées de travail. Les temps de déplacements, les frais de déplacement et d'hébergement seront traités par les sociétés d'origine des participants selon les règles en vigueur dans celles-ci,

- les participants feront parvenir au secrétariat de la commission (MT. CHARREL BSN-Groupe), dans leur langue, avant le 18 mai 1990, les points qu'ils souhaitent voir inscrits à l'ordre du jour de la réunion de Séville. Cet ordre du jour, sur lequel seront indiqués pour chaque point les sigles des syndicats qui auront demandé son inscription, sera adressé aux participants dans la première semaine de juin,

- dans toute la mesure du possible, des documents, permettant des comparaisons entre sociétés, seront envoyés aux participants dans les meilleurs délais, pour leur permettre de préparer la réunion.

Je souhaite que cette commission soit un lieu d'échanges d'information fructueux pour tous les participants.

Dans l'attente de vous retrouver à Séville, je vous prie de croire, Monsieur, en mes sentiments les meilleurs.

Jacques DEMARTY

Translation of letter to human resources managers within BSN, dated 24 April 1990

Dear Sir

As agreed at our meeting on 3 April 1990, I am writing to confirm that the general management of the packaging sector of BSN has decided to set up a <u>European glass-sector information committee</u>. This follows a request from the French CGT and the Spanish CNT unions and consultations on 3 April 1990 with the representatives of unions from BSN's glass companies in Spain, Holland and France.

The committee will enable members to receive and exchange information on the position of the companies within the sector of both an economic nature (such as financial results, market reports, industrial plans and technological innovation) and a social or industrial relations nature (including working conditions, safety and training). In no sense will the committee be a negotiating body nor will it be allowed to encroach on the representative bodies already existing within the company.

Initially, this experiment will be conducted as follows:

1. The members of the committee will include representatives of the general management of the packaging sector plus the 12 people nominated by their unions for the 3 April meeting. If necessary, another member of the same union may participate as a substitute provided that they are also employed by one of the glass companies within the BSN group and that the human resources manager of their company is notified in advance.

2. The first meeting of the committee will take place in Seville on 10 October 1990. During the afternoon of 9 October, the 12 trade union members taking part in the meeting may hold a preparatory meeting of their own. Interpreters will be made available.

3. The time spent attending the meeting will be considered as normal working time. Pay for periods of absence and the cost of travel and accommodation will be dealt with by the participants' own companies according to local custom and practice.

4. By 18 May 1990, participants will submit the points they would like included on the agenda to the secretariat of the committee (Mt. Charrel, BSN group). These may be submitted in their own language. The agenda, marked with the union requesting the inclusion of each item, will be sent to participants in the first week of June.

5. As far as possible, documents enabling comparisons to be made between companies will be sent to participants as early as possible to assist with preparations for the meeting.

It is my hope that this committee will prove to be a fruitful opportunity for the exchange of information to the benefit of all participants.

Looking forward to seeing you in Seville, I remain

yours sincerely

(Jacques Demarty)

COMMON VIEWPOINT BSN/IUF

Following the work achieved by the IUF's affiliates and the management of the BSN group during several meetings, the two parties agree that it is necessary to develop various coordinated initiatives to promote in BSN establishments, taking into account national legislation and collective agreements:

1. A policy for training for skills in order to anticipate the consequences of the introduction of new technologies or industrial restructuring. To achieve this objective, the social partners will seek to integrate this aspect into present and future plans for training.

2. A policy aiming to achieve the same level and the same quality of information, both in the economic and the social fields, in all locations of BSN subsidiaries. To achieve this objective, the social partners concerned will seek, both through national legislation as well as collective agreement, to reduce the differences observed in terms of the information between one country and another or between one location and another.

3. A development of conditions to assure real equality between men and women at work. Developing jobs and work processes have led to distortions between the situation of men and women; the social partners will therefore evaluate, location by location, the nature of the different initiatives to be adopted to improve the situation.

4. The implementation of trade union rights as defined in ILO Conventions Nos. 87, 98 and 135. The social partners concerned will identify where progress can be made in improving trade union rights and access to trade union education.

These basic principles are not exclusive; they represent the themes on which the management of BSN and the affiliates of the IUF have decided on which to jointly work.

Geneva, August 23, 1988

For BSN

Director of Human Resources
Antoine Martin

For the IUF

General Secretary
Dan Gallin

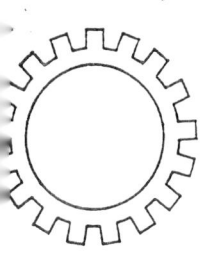

FEM Fédération Européenne des Métallurgistes dans la Communauté

EMB Europäischer Metallgewerkschaftsbund in der Gemeinschaft

EMF European Metalworkers' Federation in the Community

Adresse télégraphique EUROMETAL
Téléphone : 217.27.47
Telefax : 217.59.63

1000 BRUXELLES
rue Fossé-aux-Loups 38, (Boîte 4)

EMF POSITION PAPER
ON WORKERS' INFORMATION RIGHTS
IN MULTINATIONAL COMPANIES

1. In the light of the new opportunities that completion of the internal market provides for multinational companies, the unions affiliated to the EMF consider it necessary to set up European-level information and consultation bodies for worker representatives of firms with manufacturing operations in several countries.

    It is therefore necessary in this respect to seek negotiations with the top management of multinational companies with a view to concluding company agreements.

2. The role of these information bodies is to complement similar bodies existing at national level. Under no circumstances should they replace the latter. The national rights of worker representatives in the various countries will remain unchanged.

3. Worker representatives' rights with regard to information, consultation and exerting influence on decisions have to be defined. Full and detailed information must be provided and consultations must take place prior to decisions being taken. Real influence is to be obtained in relation to the solution of problems affecting the workers' interests.

    A) The right to information covers the following areas:-

    . The firm's economic and financial position
    . Production and sales
    . Marketing strategies
    . Production and investment programmes

    B) The right to consultation covers the following areas:-

    . Rationalisation plans

- Manufacturing and working methods
- Plant cutbacks or closures
- Plant transfers
- Changes in company organisation or company aims
- Acquisition, sale or merger of companies or plants
- Other developments or plans which may substantially affect employees

C) Procedure in the event of disagreement is to be laid down:-

If measures likely to affect the interests of the workforce in more than one country are being contemplated, the European information body should be consulted before any decision is taken.

Should this body perceive any adverse effects for the workforce, any decision shall be postponed for a pre-determined period, at its request, in order to allow time for a compromise to be worked out, if necessary with the assistance of experts specially called in for this purpose.

4. Worker representatives on the European information body shall be elected/appointed from the workforce of the different plants and belong to a trade union organisation which is recognised as being representative at national level.

The allocation of seats will be in proportion to the number of employees per plant.

The members of this body will be entitled to be accompanied by trade union experts from outside the company. (The latter are to be appointed by the members of the EMF delegation.)

5. This body shall meet at least once a year. Further meetings may take place at the request of the top management or a majority of the worker representatives.

The latter shall be entitled to organise preparatory meetings (including preparatory meetings for the EMF delegation).

All costs incurred in relation to these meetings will be met by the company.

BT/LV July 4
29th July 1988

(FIET)

MODEL AGREEMENT

Introduction

In line with the policy of the Company to develop a constructive dialogue with trade unions and employees in the countries where the Company operates, the undersigned agree to establish a European Information Committee.

Purpose

The European Information Committee is established with the purpose of developing a social dialogue between the Company and FIET.

The Committee is intended to promote regular consultation on issues of mutual concern.

The Committee will provide an opportunity for the Company and FIET to establish regular contact to exchange views and information on commercial, financial and structural developments in the Company and its subsidiaries.

Composition

The European Information Committee will be composed as follows:

- representatives of management of the Company and its subsidiaries;
- representatives of FIET and its affiliates which are organising in the Company and its subsidiaries.

Procedure

The Committee will meet at least once a year at the initiative of the Company or FIET. With the agreement of both parties the Committee may meet on an ad-hoc basis.

The venue for the meeting will be chosen by the Company and the Company will also be responsible for the payment of the following costs:

- travel and accommodation costs of participants;
- meeting room and interpretation expenses.

Functions

The Committee shall be informed of the commercial, financial and structural developments in the Company. The Company will report on plans and investments in technology and the implications of this on its organisational structure. The Committee should also be informed of measures taken and planned which will involve major structural and commercial changes in the Company.

Confidentiality

Members of the Committee undertake to respect the confidential nature of any documents that are submitted for discussion.

Duration

This agreement is concluded for an indeterminate period.

APPENDIX III : Current Situation at Airbus, CIS, Ford, Gillette, IBC and Unilever

This Appendix consists of a brief account of the current situation in the six remaining companies in our survey (Airbus, Gillette, Unilever, CIS, Ford and IBC) whose details were not included in Section 2 of this report since there are no joint arrangements in force in the first three, and there are only joint visits at Ford and IBC.

Arrangements at CIS take place at European sectoral level, through the Association of European Cooperative Insurers.

Clearly, these developments fall short of the focus of this report on MNCs, so we reproduce instead the details here outside its main body.

Airbus

As a company registered in France, Airbus is required under French law to have a works council to represent the interests of its 600 directly recruited employees. Serious problems have arisen, however, in relation to the representation of its 600 seconded employees. The European Metalworkers' Federation has drawn up - to our knowledge - four drafts of an agreement for an Airbus Industrie Staff Council, the latest of which is dated 4 October 1990.

Representatives, who would be elected to the Staff Council through electoral colleges based on each of the four partner companies, would exercise rights to consultation and information on specified subjects.

However, management continues to refuse to meet the unions since representation of internationally seconded employees falls outside the scope of French labour law, and it alleges that, were a Staff Council set up, they would acquire a dual set of rights. For example, a German employee would have the normal rights granted through domestic German works council legislation in Deutsche Airbus but would then also acquire rights as a seconded employee at Airbus Industrie in France.

The dispute to gain recognition has been the subject of a protracted legal case in the courts in Bordeaux. At the time of writing (October 1991) there is still no sign of an outcome.

Category: no transnational joint meetings.

Cooperative Insurance Society

The Association of European Cooperative Insurers (AECI), which represents cooperative insurance companies in Austria, Belgium, Germany, Italy, Sweden and the UK, has been meeting the insurance trade section of Euro-FIET on a regular, annual basis since 1979, normally in April. The British company within the AECI is the Cooperative Insurance Society, the Germany company is Volksfürsorge, the Swedish company is Folksam and so on. This is a sectoral arrangement between AECI and Euro-FIET, with the added dimension that the latter also regularly meets DG XV of the Commission, the Directorate General responsible for the insurance and finance aspects of the single European market.

There is no formal agreement between AECI and Euro-FIET in this area, but the two sides have concluded two statements on best practice: one covers technology in the cooperative insurance sector (areas such as participation, avoidance of compulsory redundancies, working conditions and training), whilst the other covers equality for women in cooperative insurance (including recruitment, pay, training and development).

Around ten managers attend - though their seniority varies by country, they include general and personnel managers. There are fifteen union representatives, including representation from Euro-FIET.

Category: agreed practice at European sector level.

Ford

The German and UK product development centres within Ford have been jointly responsible for car development and so, in 1978, the German metalworkers' union, IG Metall, funded a joint meeting for its UK opposite number, TASS (now MSF).

These meetings continued for some years on roughly a quarterly basis. Management knew about the meetings, but did not participate. The UK unions have a monthly meeting with their local management and a quarterly meeting with senior management some of which have been attended by works council representatives from Cologne.

In addition, there have been exchange visits between German and UK unions with management to assess particular problems - for example, one visit to investigate the problem of noise, vibration and harshness in product development was followed up by a study group and report. Local management favours these consultative meetings on technical issues, but since September 1990, when reorganisation of the product development centre took place, there has been pressure to run down exchange visits (and replace them by conference video facilities).

IG Metall has produced its own draft agreement for a European Works Council within Ford, although the prospects for its establishment are considered slim.

Category: joint exchange visits

Gillette

An international coordination committee was formed by the unions operating within Gillette in Europe in 1988 - the committee is known by its French acronym, GISEL (Gillette Inter-Syndicale Européenne de Liaison).

The factors which prompted its formation at that point included the reorganisation of working time within the company, such as the introduction of weekend working in the UK which concerned employees in Germany and Spain, and the campaign to prevent the closure of the Gillette plant at Annecy in France. French, German and Spanish unions signed the GISEL agreement in February 1989, joined in 1990 by Italian and UK unions.

Two annual conferences have been held so far - in Annecy (1989) and in Berlin (1990). At least one works councillor attends from each country and the presidency rotates between the countries. Management has been hostile to this initiative from the outset and refuses to meet GISEL.

Category: no transnational joint meetings.

IBC Vehicles

In the late 1970s and 1980s when the Luton factory - now owned by IBC - was part of Vauxhall annual exchange visits took place with the Opel engine plants in Germany. These visits continued when General Motors took over, but they died out around 1984/85.

In 1985 the Transnational Information Exchange Group organised a meeting of shop stewards and their equivalents across all General Motors plants. In 1987, Isuzu took a 40% stake in the company to form IBC Vehicles - General Motors held the remaining 60%.

In September 1989 an Austrian delegation, which included both management representatives and works councillors from the General Motors plant at Aspen, visited the Luton plant to discuss the recently revamped industrial relations system, known as the Isuzu Production System.

In January 1990 the five senior union representatives, accompanied by four management representatives from IBC, paid a return visit to Aspen where they discussed conditions of employment in Austria (sickness benefit, job grading, pensions, participation, and so on) as well as other technical issues on which consultation took place. No strategic management subjects were discussed as there is no common corporate strategy involving the two plants. Further exchange visits to Japan and Spain also took place in 1990.

Category: joint exchange visits.

Unilever

Following restructuring in Van den Berghs in the margarine division of Unilever's food sector, two meetings took place in 1989 of union representatives across the company's European operations - one for the food sector and the other for the chemicals sector. Then on 11 April 1990 the ECF/IUF and EFCGU jointly coordinated a European Unilever Conference, with support from DGV of the Commission, which agreed the composition of a Unilever European Group Committee to bring together unions representing workers across both sectors on a regular basis. A second meeting took place in Luxembourg in June 1991.

Management has been hostile to this initiative from the outset and refuses to meet the unions' European Group Committee.

Category: no transnational joint meetings.

APPENDIX IV : Methodology

This report is based on 35 interviews across five countries with management, unions and employee representatives in the following companies :-

> Airbus, Allianz, BSN, Bull, Cooperative Insurance Society, Ford, Gillette, IBC, Nestlé, Péchiney, Rhône-Poulenc, St Gobain, Thomson Consumer Electronics, Unilever and Volkswagen.

The interviews were based on a standard questionnaire and carried out mainly by telephone between November 1990 and March 1991. During the interview, the interviewer took notes which were then read into a cassette recorder. The cassettes were subsequently transcribed for the purposes of analysis.

There were three interviews in Belgium, three in the Irish Republic, nine in France, nine in Germany and eleven in the UK. Of the total, seven were with management, though a further six managers declined to be interviewed. Reasons given included the fact that the staff council was not yet operative (Airbus); lack of time (Allianz); the fact that only French managers take part (German manager at BSN); no reason given (BSN); instruction required from Swiss HQ (Nestlé); and 'inappropriateness' of the questions as the company is decentralised (Unilever).

Whilst we asked just over 50 separate questions, they were conveniently grouped for the purposes of this report under eight principal headings :-

> origins of the initiatives; representation; operational aspects; benefits to management; benefits to employee representatives; negative experiences; future development; and preconditions for effectiveness.

In Section 2, which analyses in detail the structural aspects of a number of European-level information/consultation arrangements, we have focused principally on those on which written material (agreements, exchanges of letters and so on) has been available to us. This is because interview material is not always totally reliable when it comes to analysing objective information like procedures or structures - memory is not always the best witness to the numbers of representatives on a committee, the names of the unions involved, or the topics discussed at a meeting up to a year ago (though, naturally, for the evaluation of subjective assessments of practice, in Section 3, the interview material comes into its own). Written documentation, in short, lacks the ambiguity of recall, and for this reason it forms the foundation for our discussion of structures, whether formal or not. Indeed, such a firm foundation is particularly important as on it we identify the key characteristics of a basic model for European-level information and consultation bodies within MNCs.

The authors gratefully acknowledge the contributions of the interviewers :-

Dirk Buda (interviews in Germany); Kevin O'Kelly (Ireland); and Lydia Zaïd (Belgium and France). Michael Gold conducted the UK interviews.

In addition, Kevin O'Kelly interviewed representatives of the following organisations :-

Employers/Industry
Union of Industrial and Employers' Confederations of Europe (UNICE); Council of European Chemical Federations (CEFIC); and the Western European Metal Trades Employers' Organisations.

Unions
European Trade Union Confederation (ETUC); European Federation of Chemical and General Workers' Unions (EFCGU); European Regional Organisation of the International Federation of Commercial, Clerical and Technical Employees (Euro-FIET); European Committee of Food, Catering and Allied Workers' Unions within the IUF (ECF/IUF); and the European Metalworkers' Federation in the Community (EMF).

We also record our thanks to the many people who agreed to be interviewed and who took the time and trouble to give us leads and information. The staff of Words on Wheels, Twickenham, produced this report with efficiency and good humour.

European Communities—Commission

European-level Information and Consultation in Multinational Companies—
An Evaluation of Practice

Luxembourg: Office for Official Publications of the European Communities

1992—134p.—160 × 235mm

ISBN 92-826-3714-X

Catalogue Number: SY-73-91-522-EN-C

Price (excluding VAT) in Luxembourg: ECU 11.25

Venta y suscripciones • Salg og abonnement • Verkauf und Abonnement • Πωλήσεις και συνδρομές
Sales and subscriptions • Vente et abonnements • Vendita e abbonamenti
Verkoop en abonnementen • Venda e assinaturas

BELGIQUE / BELGIË

Moniteur belge /
Belgisch Staatsblad
Rue de Louvain 42 / Leuvenseweg 42
1000 Bruxelles / 1000 Brussel
Tél. (02) 512 00 26
Fax 511 01 84
CCP / Postrekening 000-2005502-27

Autres distributeurs /
Overige verkooppunten

Librairie européenne/
Europese Boekhandel
Avenue Albert Jonnart 50 /
Albert Jonnartlaan 50
1200 Bruxelles / 1200 Brussel
Tél. (02) 734 02 81
Fax 735 08 60

Jean De Lannoy
Avenue du Roi 202 /Koningslaan 202
1060 Bruxelles / 1060 Brussel
Tél. (02) 538 51 69
Télex 63220 UNBOOK B
Fax (02) 538 08 41

CREDOC
Rue de la Montagne 34 / Bergstraat 34
Bte 11 / Bus 11
1000 Bruxelles / 1000 Brussel

DANMARK

J. H. Schultz Information A/S
EF-Publikationer
Ottiliavej 18
2500 Valby
Tlf. 36 44 22 66
Fax 36 44 01 41
Girokonto 6 00 08 86

BR DEUTSCHLAND

Bundesanzeiger Verlag
Breite Straße
Postfach 10 80 06
5000 Köln 1
Tel. (02 21) 20 29-0
Fernschreiber:
ANZEIGER BONN 8 882 595
Fax 20 29 278

GREECE

G.C. Eleftheroudakis SA
International Bookstore
Nikis Street 4
10563 Athens
Tel. (01) 322 63 23
Telex 219410 ELEF
Fax 323 98 21

ESPAÑA

Boletin Oficial del Estado
Trafalgar, 27
28010 Madrid
Tel. (91) 44 82 135

Mundi-Prensa Libros, S.A.
Castelló, 37
28001 Madrid
Tel. (91) 431 33 99 (Libros)
       431 32 22 (Suscripciones)
       435 36 37 (Dirección)
Télex 49370-MPLI-E
Fax (91) 575 39 98

Sucursal:

Libreria Internacional AEDOS
Consejo de Ciento, 391
08009 Barcelona
Tel. (93) 301 86 15
Fax (93) 317 01 41

Llibreria de la Generalitat
de Catalunya
Rambla dels Estudis , 118 (Palau Moja)
08002 Barcelona
Tel. (93) 302 68 35
     302 64 62
Fax 302 12 99

FRANCE

Journal officiel
Service des publications
des Communautés européennes
26, rue Desaix
75727 Paris Cedex 15
Tél. (1) 40 58 75 00
Fax (1) 40 58 75 74

IRELAND

Government Publications
Sales Office
Sun Alliance House
Molesworth Street
Dublin 2
Tel. 71 03 09

or by post

Government Stationery Office
EEC Section
6th floor
Bishop Street
Dublin 8
Tel. 78 16 66
Fax 78 06 45

ITALIA

Licosa Spa
Via Benedetto Fortini, 120/10
Casella postale 552
50125 Firenze
Tel. (055) 64 54 15
Fax 64 12 57
Telex 570466 LICOSA I
CCP 343 509

Subagenti:

Libreria scientifica
Lucio de Biasio - AEIOU
Via Meravigli, 16
20123 Milano
Tel. (02) 80 76 79

Herder Editrice e Libreria
Piazza Montecitorio, 117-120
00186 Roma
Tel. (06) 679 46 28/679 53 04

Libreria giuridica
Via XII Ottobre, 172/R
16121 Genova
Tel. (010) 59 56 93

GRAND-DUCHÉ DE LUXEMBOURG

Abonnements seulement
Subscriptions only
Nur für Abonnements

Messageries Paul Kraus
11, rue Christophe Plantin
2339 Luxembourg
Tél. 499 88 88
Télex 2515
Fax 499 88 84 44
CCP 49242-63

NEDERLAND

SDU Overheidsinformatie
Externe Fondsen
Postbus 20014
2500 EA 's-Gravenhage
Tel. (070) 37 89 911
Fax (070) 34 75 778

PORTUGAL

Imprensa Nacional
Casa da Moeda, EP
Rua D. Francisco Manuel de Melo, 5
P-1092 Lisboa Codex
Tel. (01) 69 34 14

Distribuidora de Livros
Bertrand, Ld.ª
Grupo Bertrand, SA
Rua das Terras dos Vales, 4-A
Apartado 37
P-2700 Amadora Codex
Tel. (01) 49 59 050
Telex 15798 BERDIS
Fax 49 60 255

UNITED KINGDOM

HMSO Books (PC 16)
HMSO Publications Centre
51 Nine Elms Lane
London SW8 5DR
Tel. (071) 873 9090
Fax GP3 873 8463
Telex 29 71 138

Sub-agent:

Alan Armstrong Ltd
2 Arkwright Road
Reading, Berks RG2 0SQ
Tel. (0734) 75 18 55
Telex 849937 AAALTD G
Fax (0734) 75 51 64

ÖSTERREICH

Manz'sche Verlags-
und Universitätsbuchhandlung
Kohlmarkt 16
1014 Wien
Tel. (0222) 531 61-0
Telex 11 25 00 BOX A
Fax (0222) 531 61-81

SVERIGE

BTJ
Box 200
22100 Lund
Tel. (046) 18 00 00
Fax (046) 18 01 25

SCHWEIZ / SUISSE / SVIZZERA

OSEC
Stampfenbachstraße 85
8035 Zürich
Tel. (01) 365 51 51
Fax (01) 365 54 11

MAGYARORSZÁG

Agroinform
Központ:
Budapest I., Attila út 93. H-1012

Levélcim:
Budapest, Pf.: 15 H-1253
Tel. 36 (1) 56 82 11
Telex (22) 4717 AGINF H-61

POLAND

Business Foundation
ul. Wspólna 1/3
PL-00-529 Warszawa
Tel. 48 (22) 21 99 93/21 84 20
Fax 48 (22) 28 05 49

YUGOSLAVIA

Privredni Vjesnik
Bulevar Lenjina 171/XIV
11070 - Beograd
Tel. 123 23 40

TÜRKIYE

Pres Dagitim Ticaret ve sanayi A.Ş.
Narlibahçe Sokak No. 15
Cağaloğlu
Istanbul
Tel. 512 01 90
Telex 23822 DSVO-TR

AUTRES PAYS
OTHER COUNTRIES
ANDERE LÄNDER

Office des publications officielles
des Communautés européennes
2, rue Mercier
L-2985 Luxembourg
Tél. 49 92 81
Télex PUBOF LU 1324 b
Fax 48 85 73
CC bancaire BIL 8-109/6003/700

CANADA

Renouf Publishing Co. Ltd
Mail orders — Head Office:
1294 Algoma Road
Ottawa, Ontario K1B 3W8
Tel. (613) 741 43 33
Fax (613) 741 54 39
Telex 0534783

Ottawa Store:
61 Sparks Street
Tel. (613) 238 89 85

Toronto Store:
211 Yonge Street
Tel. (416) 363 31 71

UNITED STATES OF AMERICA

UNIPUB
4611-F Assembly Drive
Lanham, MD 20706-4391
Tel. Toll Free (800) 274 4888
Fax (301) 459 0056

AUSTRALIA

Hunter Publications
58A Gipps Street
Collingwood
Victoria 3066

JAPAN

Kinokuniya Company Ltd
17-7 Shinjuku 3-Chome
Shinjuku-ku
Tokyo 160-91
Tel. (03) 3439-0121

Journal Department
PO Box 55 Chitose
Tokyo 156
Tel. (03) 3439-0124